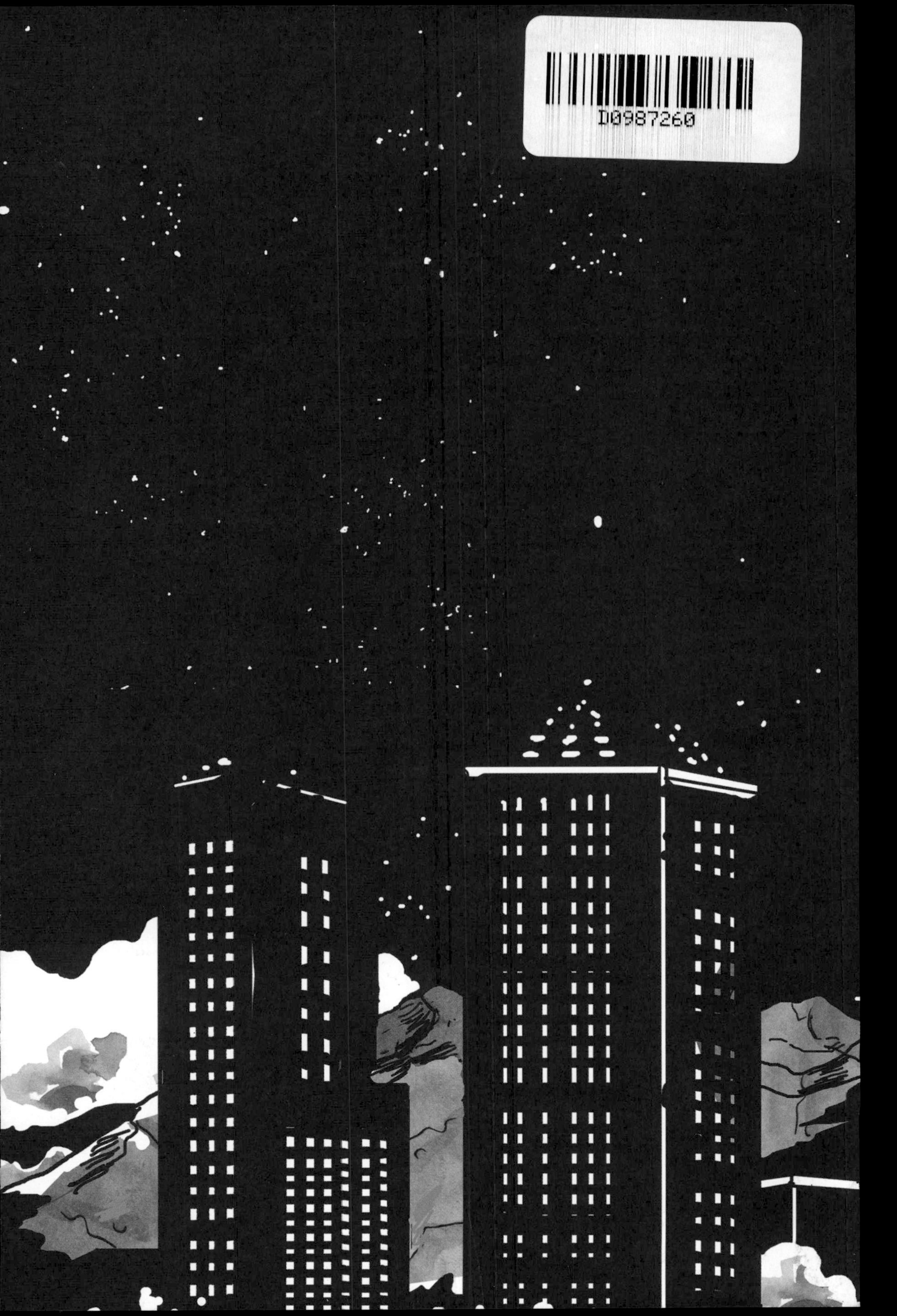

i love
this part

tillie walden

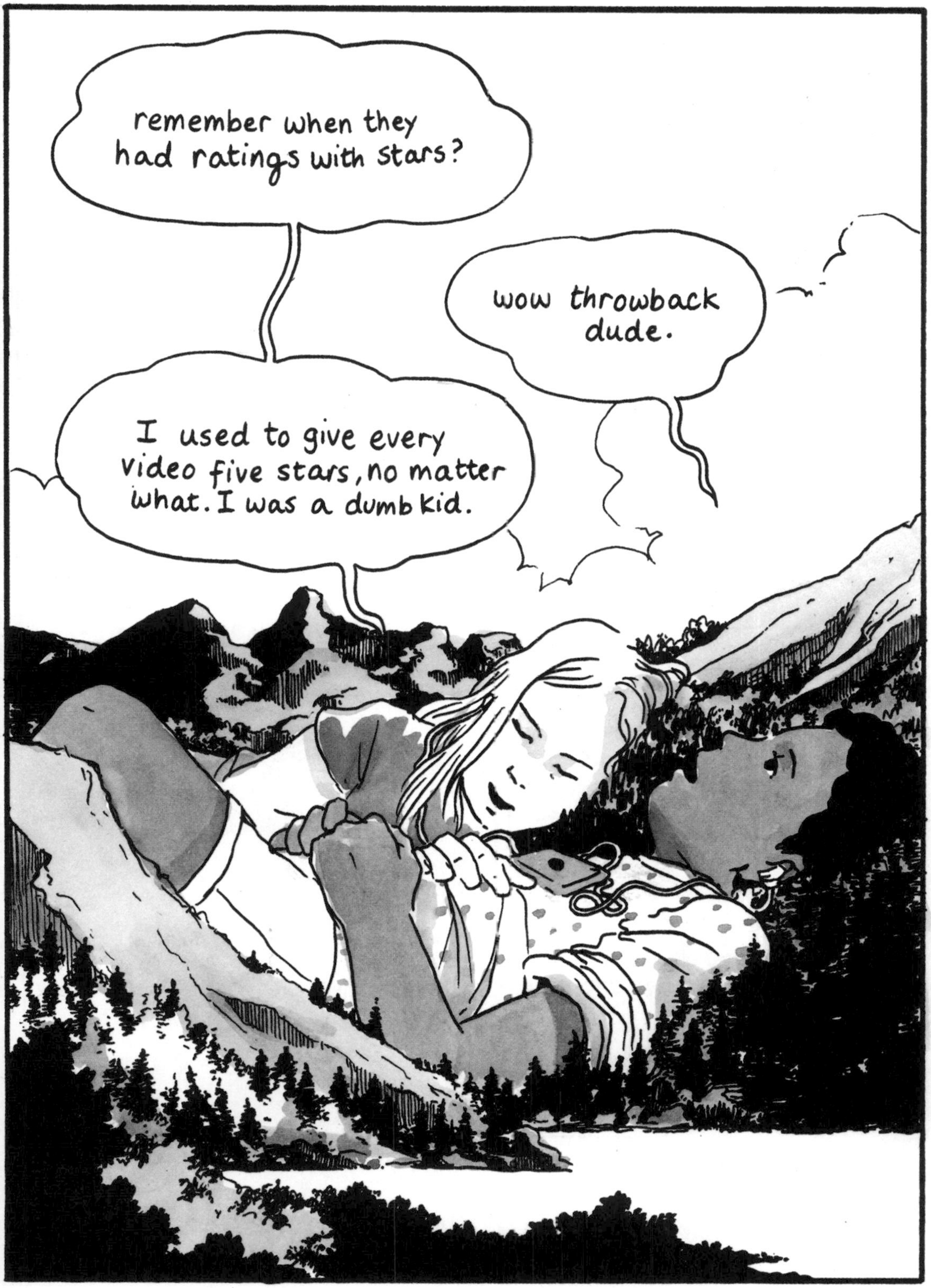
remember when they had ratings with stars?
I used to give every video five stars, no matter what. I was a dumb kid.
wow throwback dude.

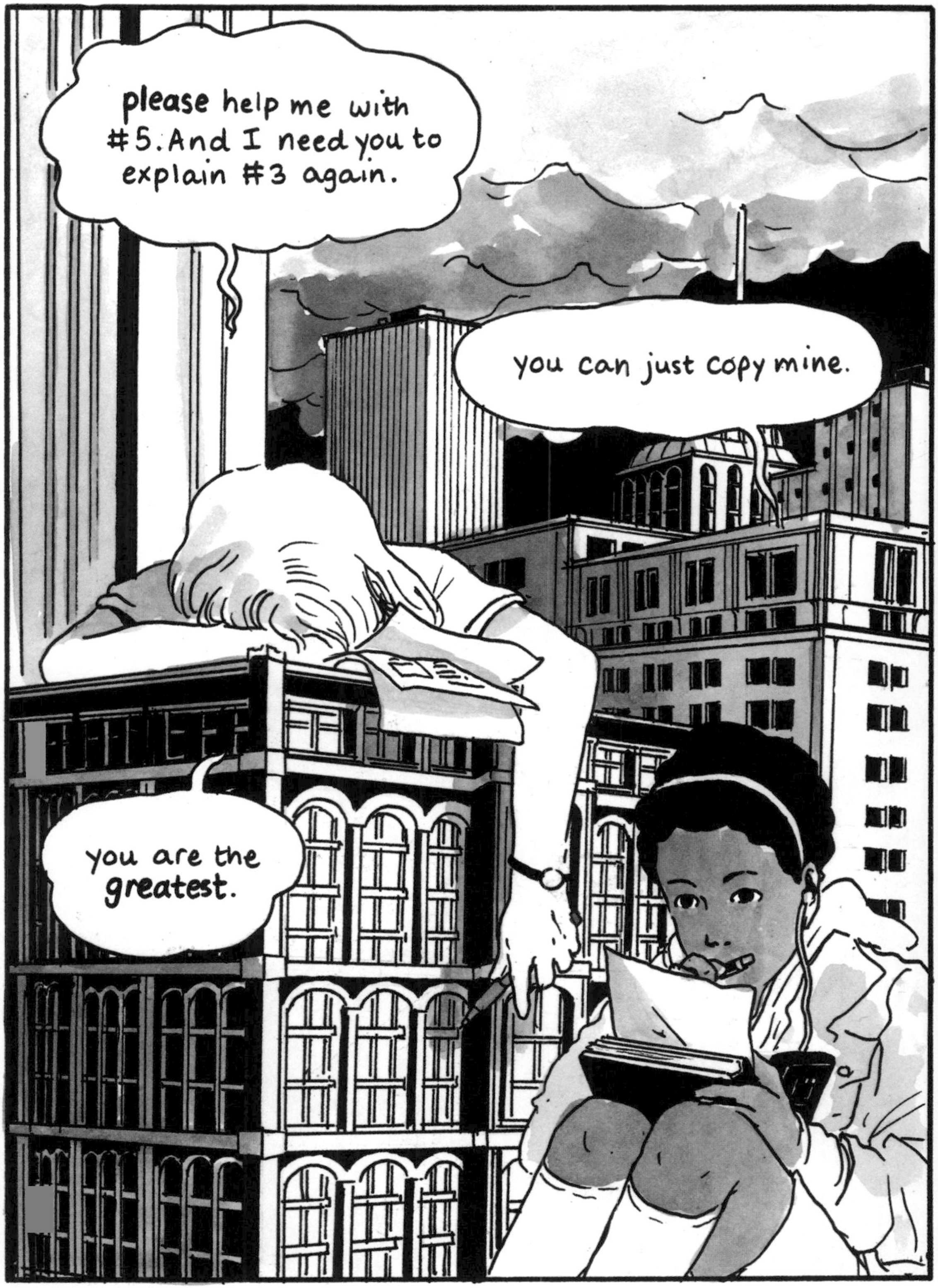
please help me with #5. And I need you to explain #3 again.
you can just copy mine.
you are the greatest.

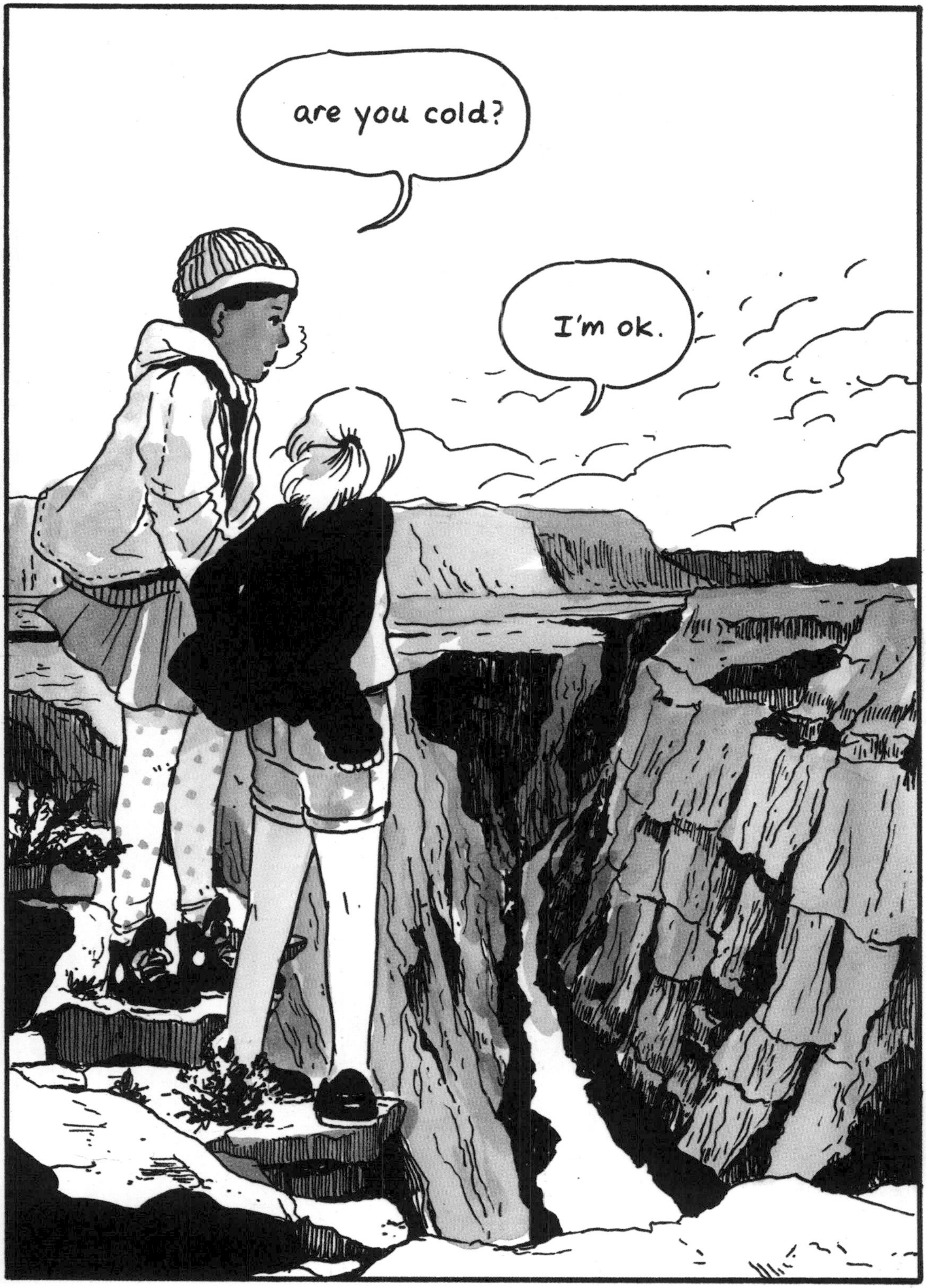
are you cold?
I'm ok.

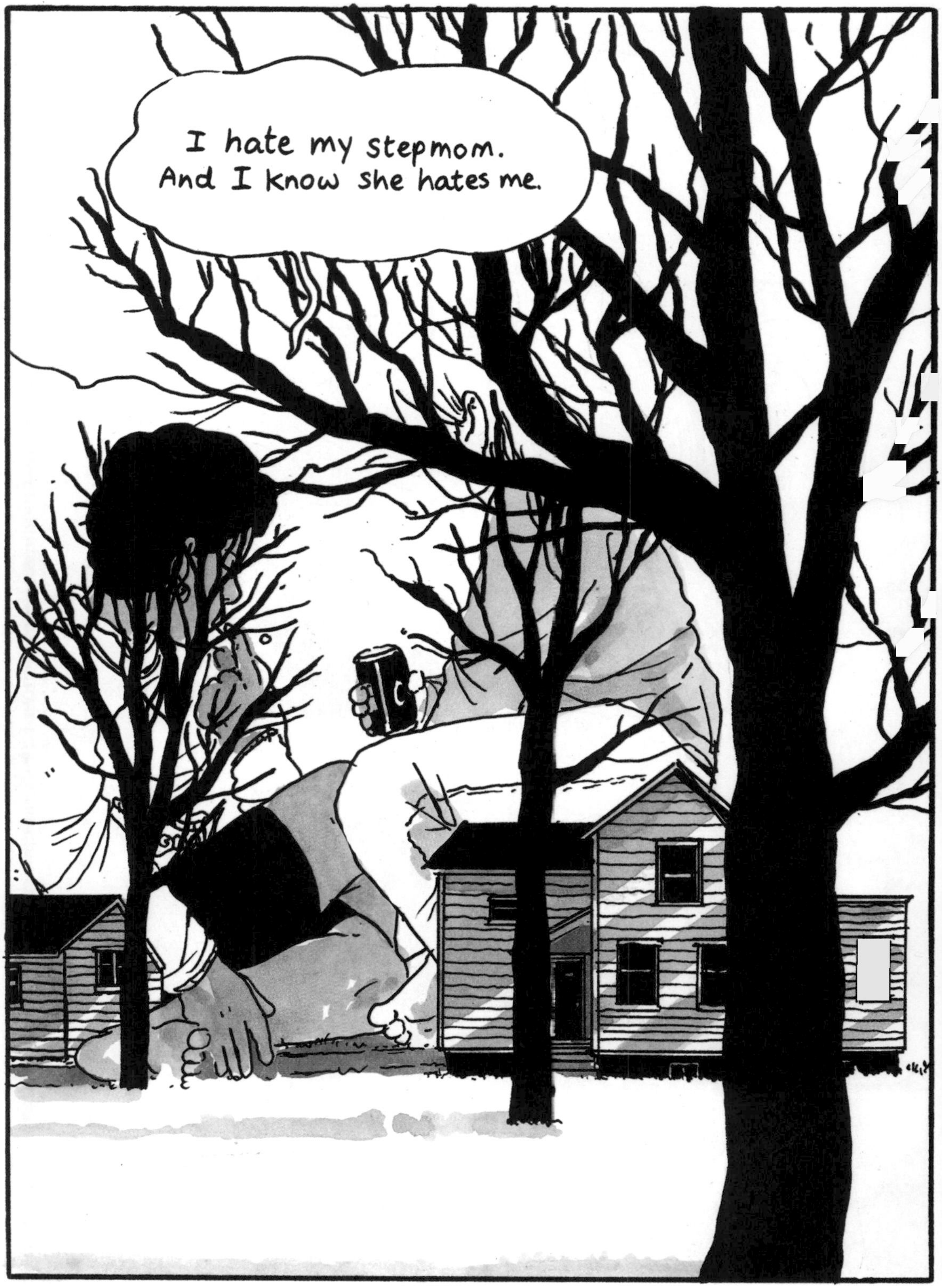
I hate my stepmom. And I know she hates me.

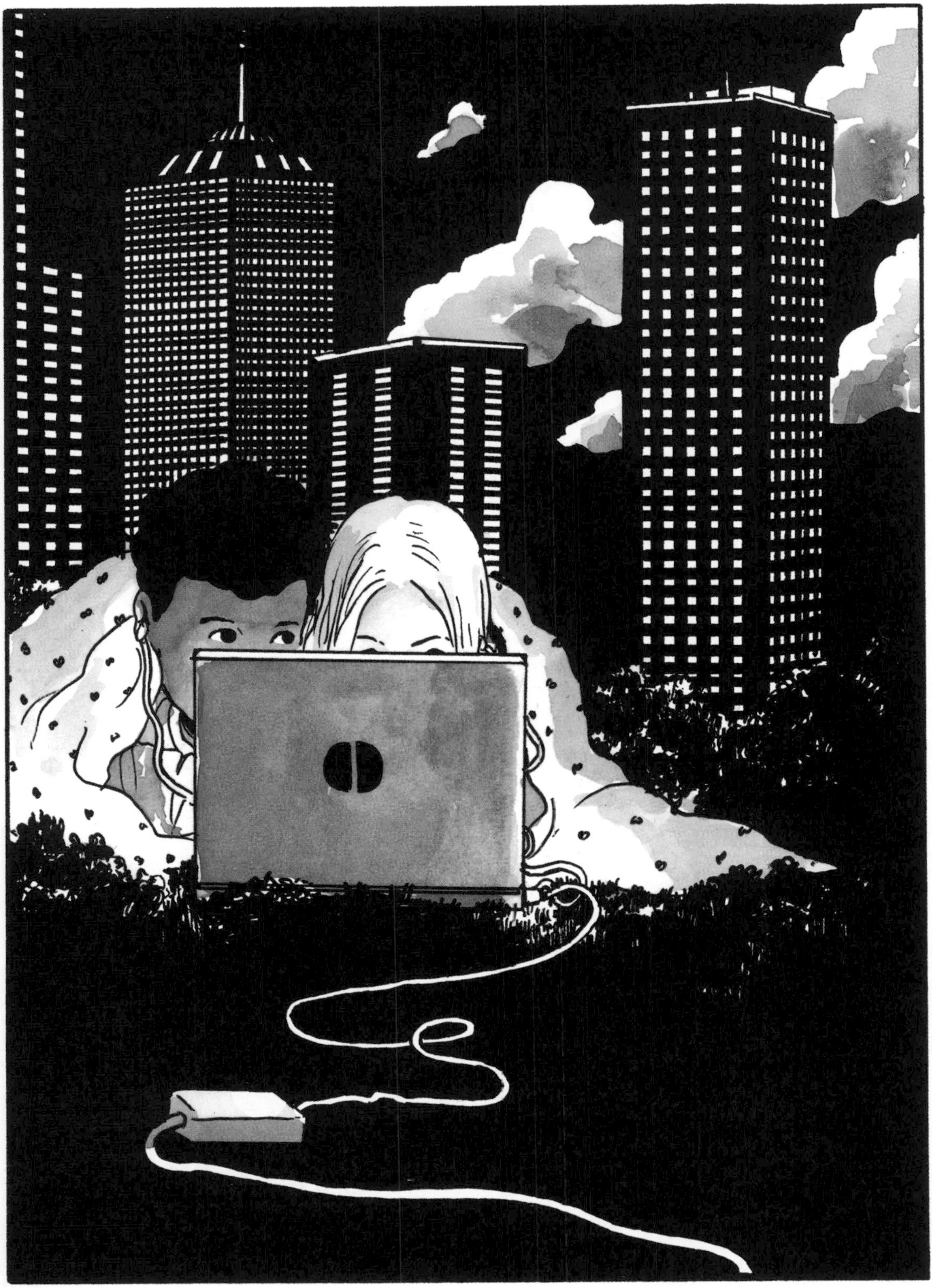

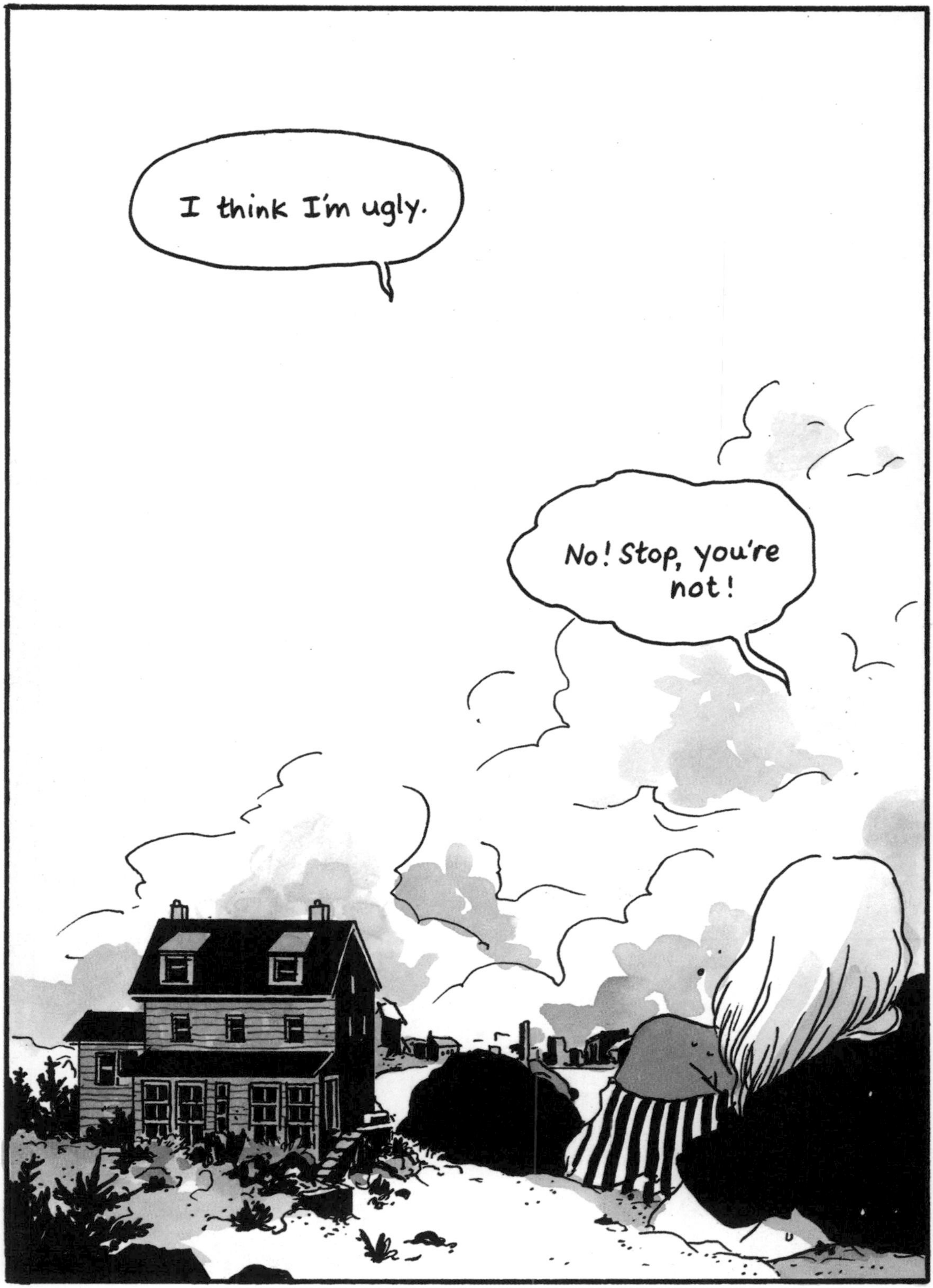
I think I'm ugly.
No! Stop, you're not!

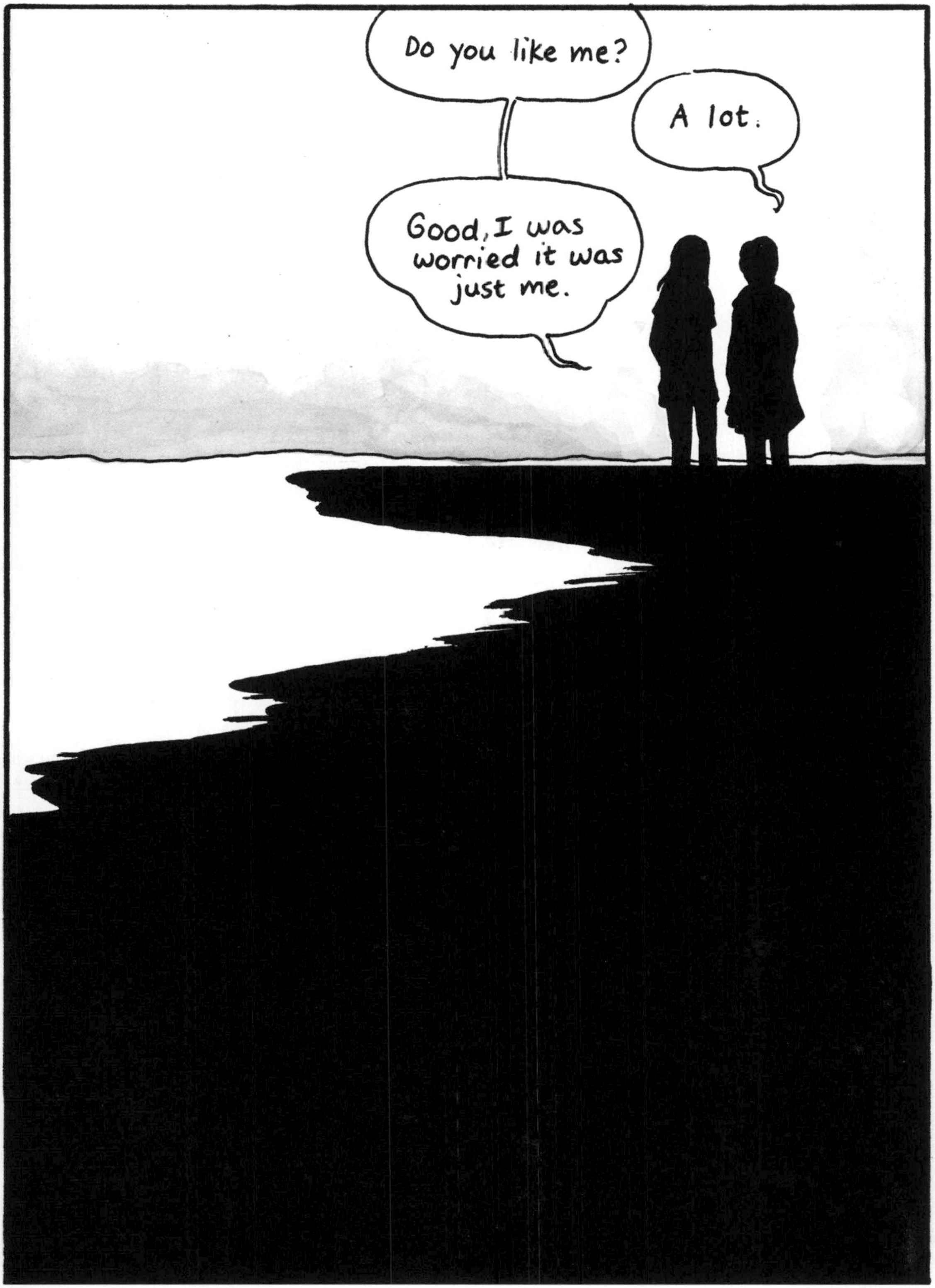
Do you like me?
A lot.
Good, I was worried it was just me.

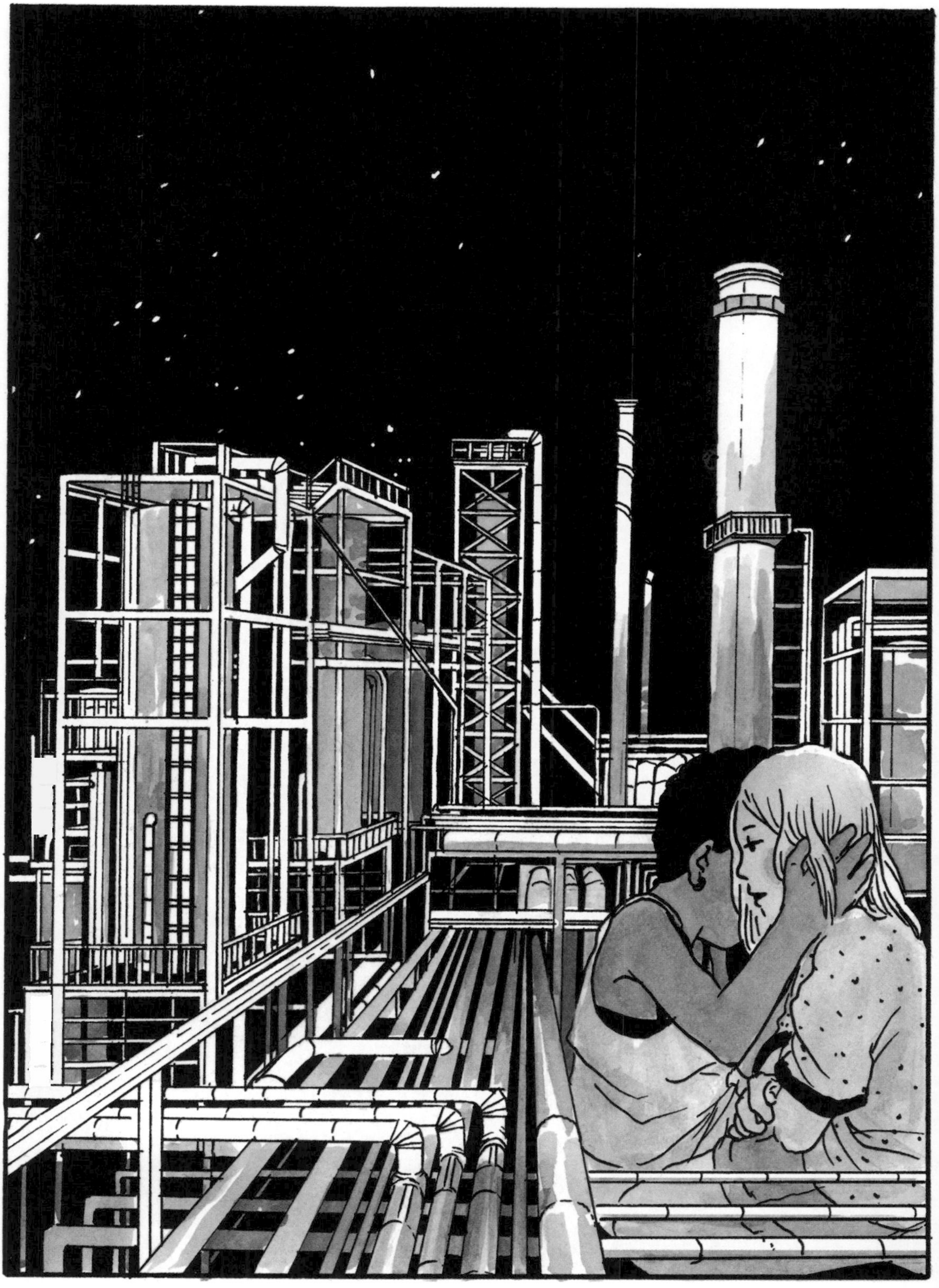

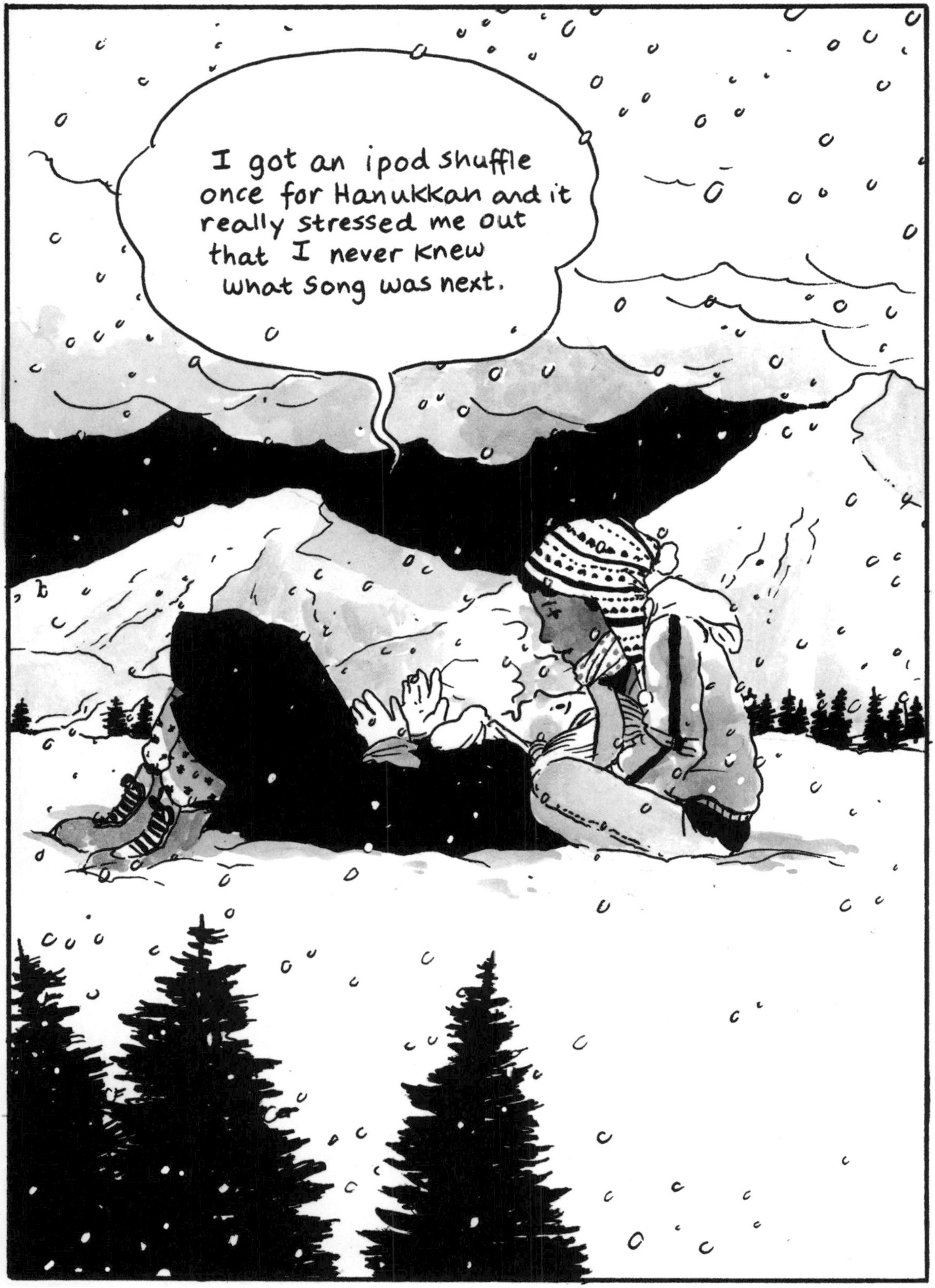
I got an ipod shuffle once for Hanukkah and it really stressed me out that I never knew what song was next.

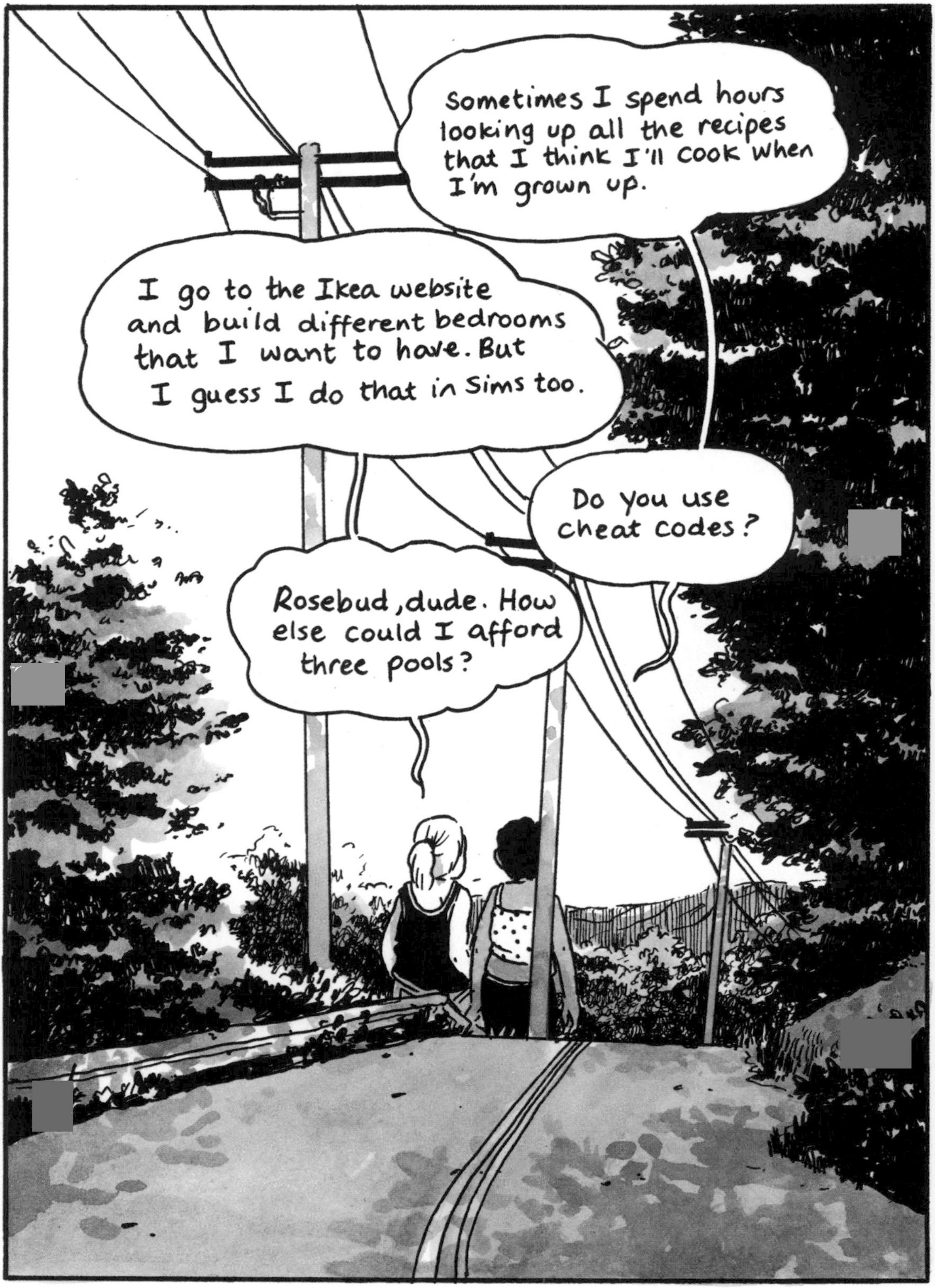
Sometimes I spend hours looking up all the recipes that I think I'll cook when I'm grown up.
I go to the Ikea website and build different bedrooms that I want to have. But I guess I do that in Sims too.
Do you use cheat codes?
Rosebud, dude. How else could I afford three pools?

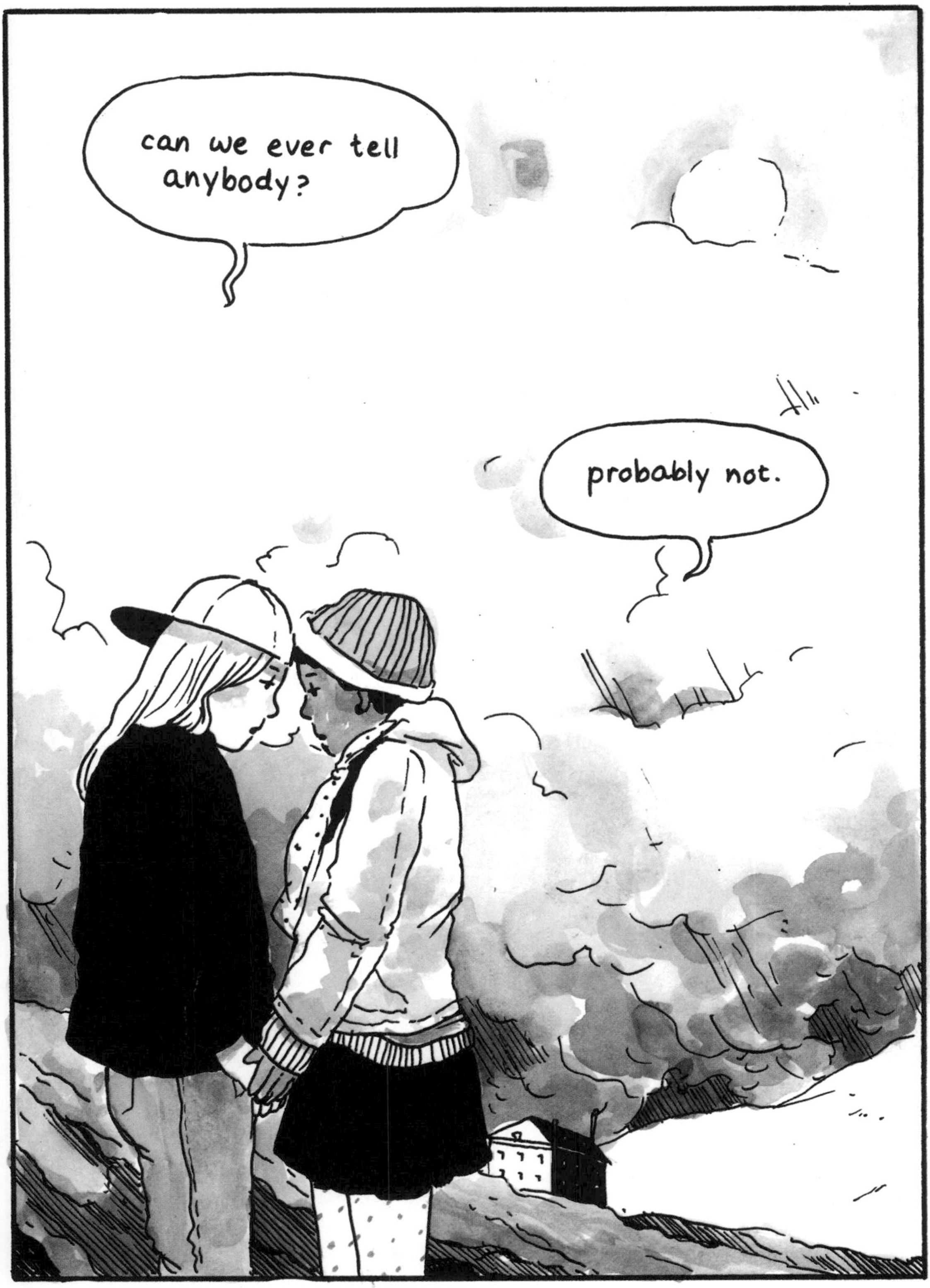
can we ever tell anybody?
probably not.

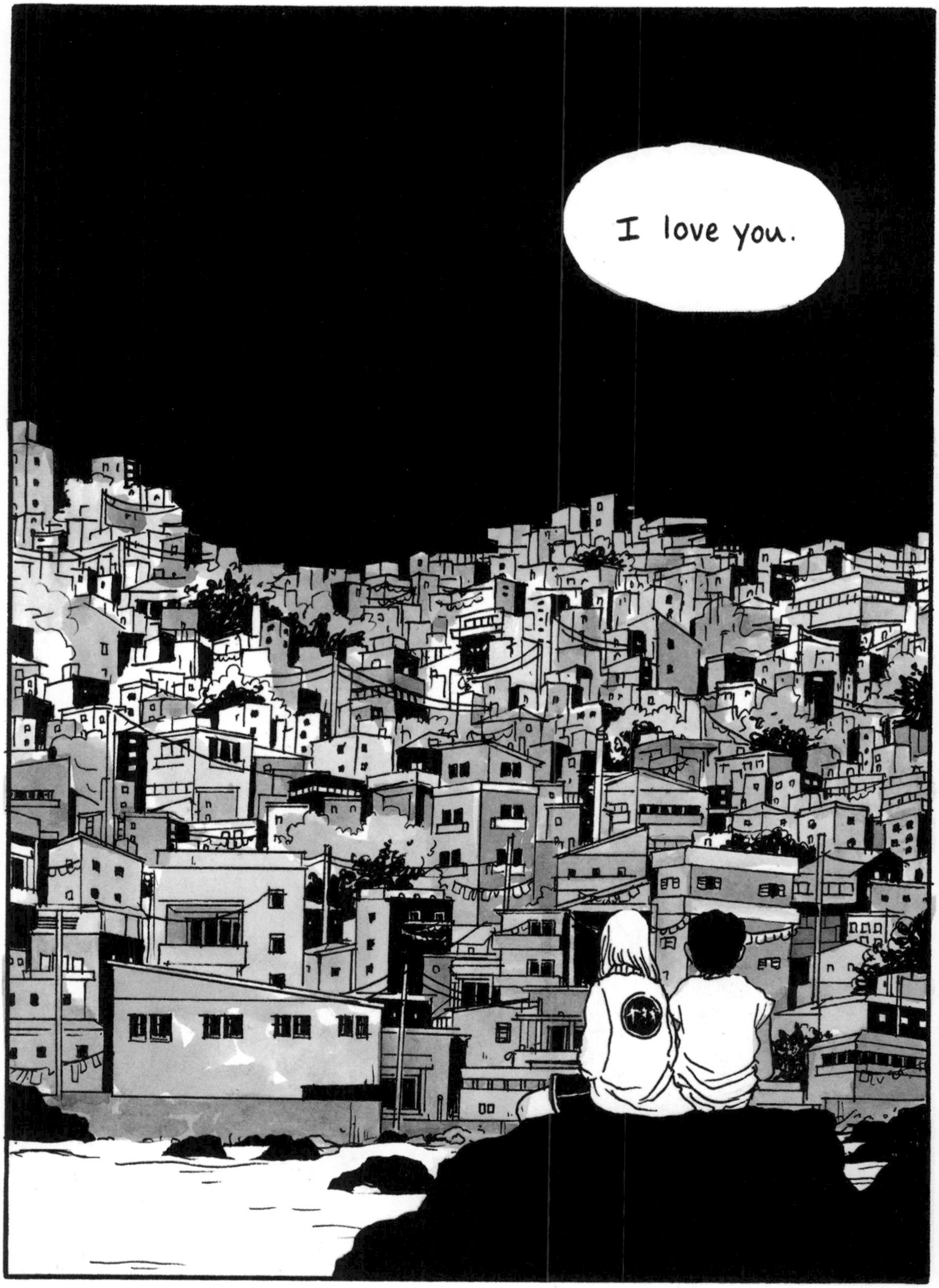
I love you.

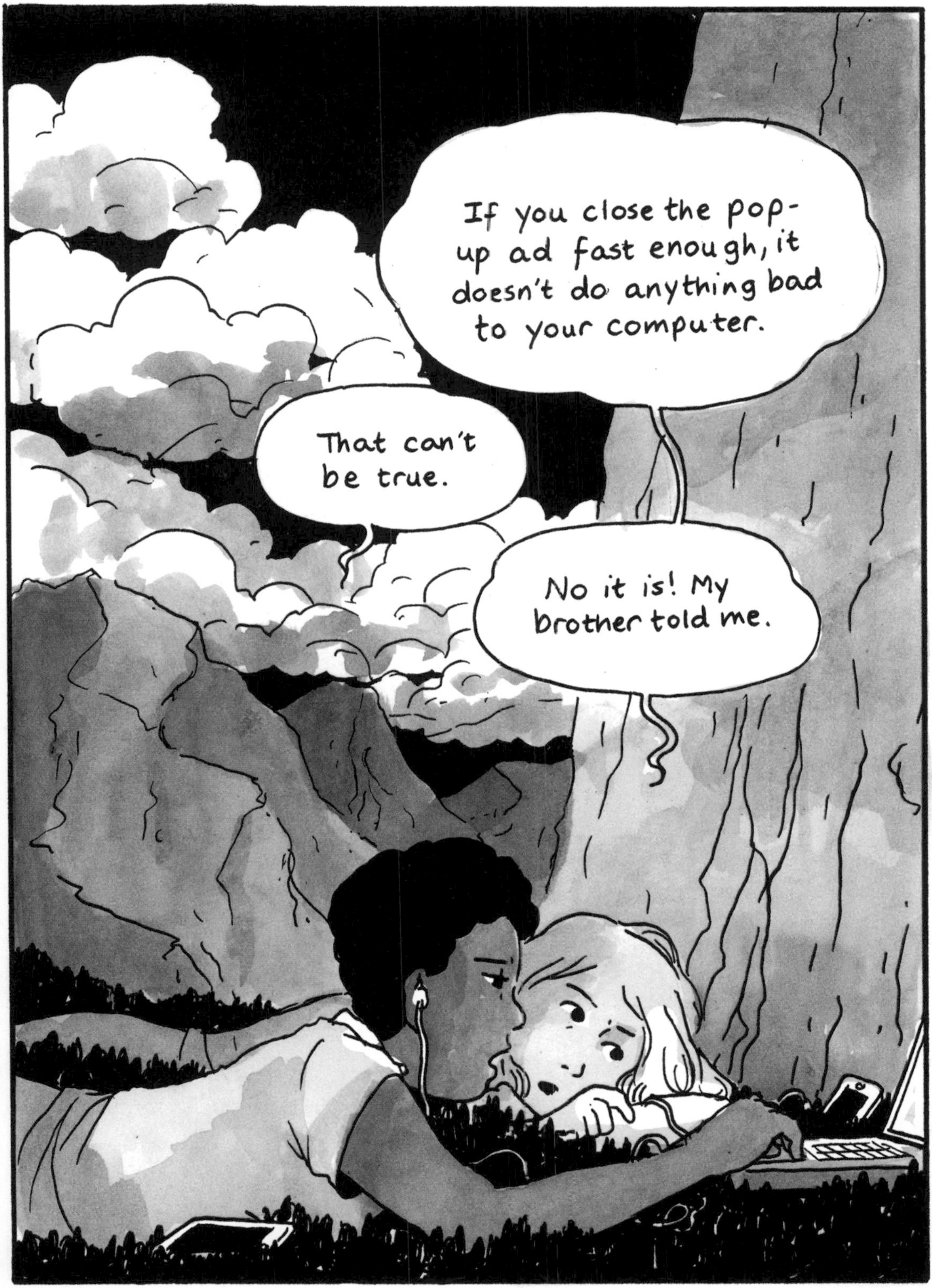
If you close the pop-up ad fast enough, it doesn't do anything bad to your computer.
That can't be true.
No it is! My brother told me.

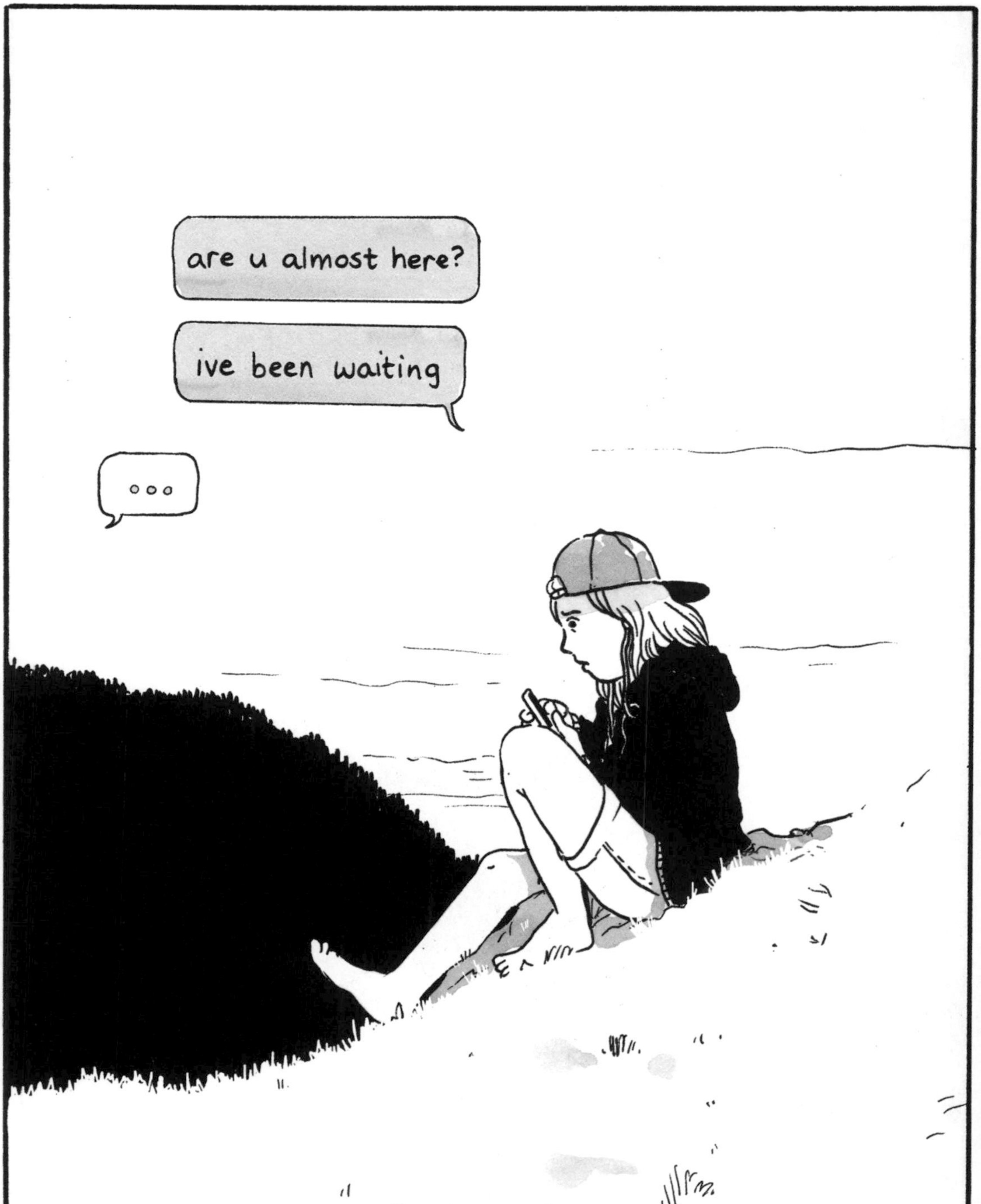
are u almost here?
ive been waiting
...

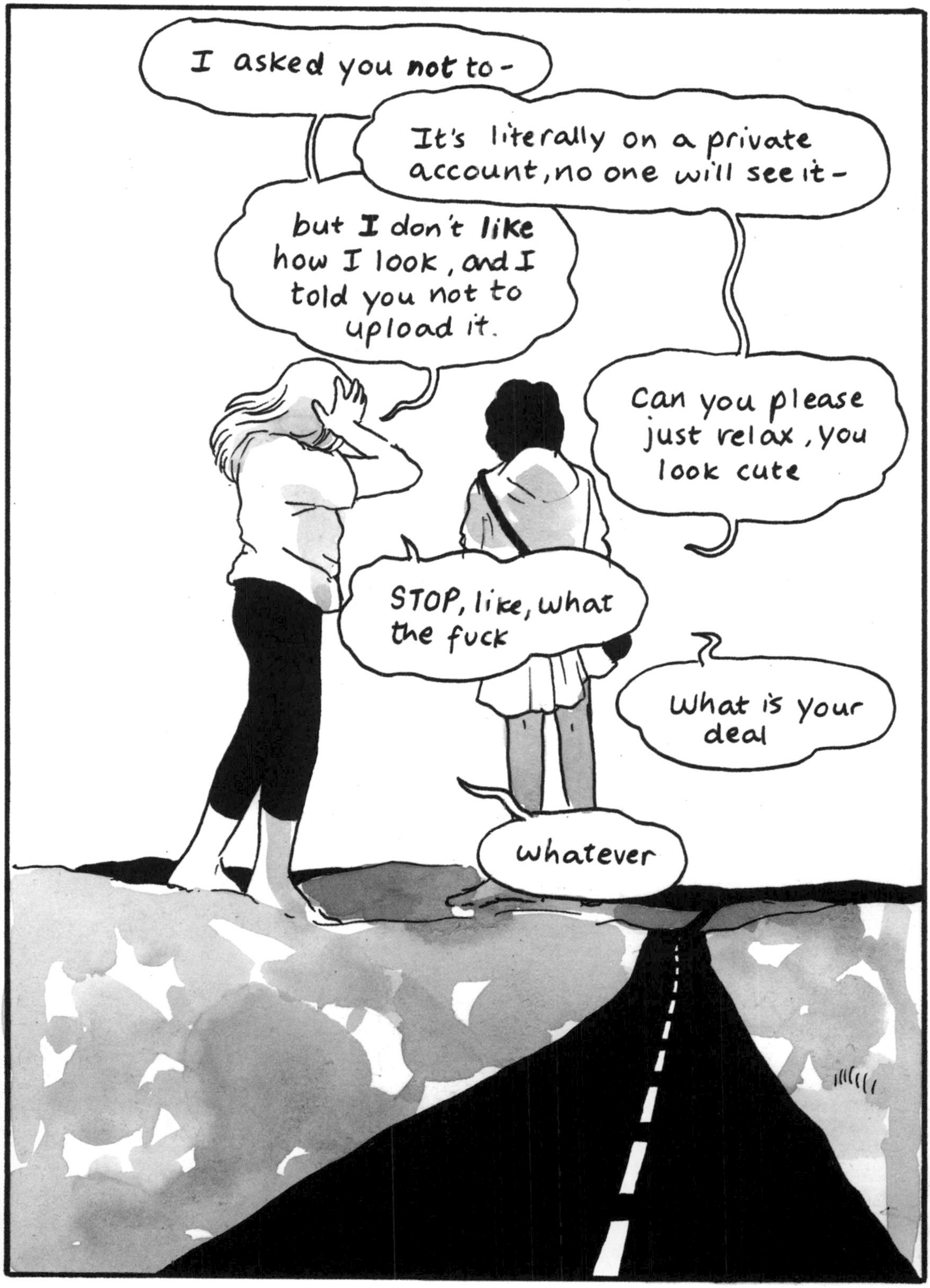
I asked you not to-
It's literally on a private account, no one will see it-
but I don't like how I look, and I told you not to upload it.
Can you please just relax, you look cute
STOP, like, what the fuck
What is your deal
whatever

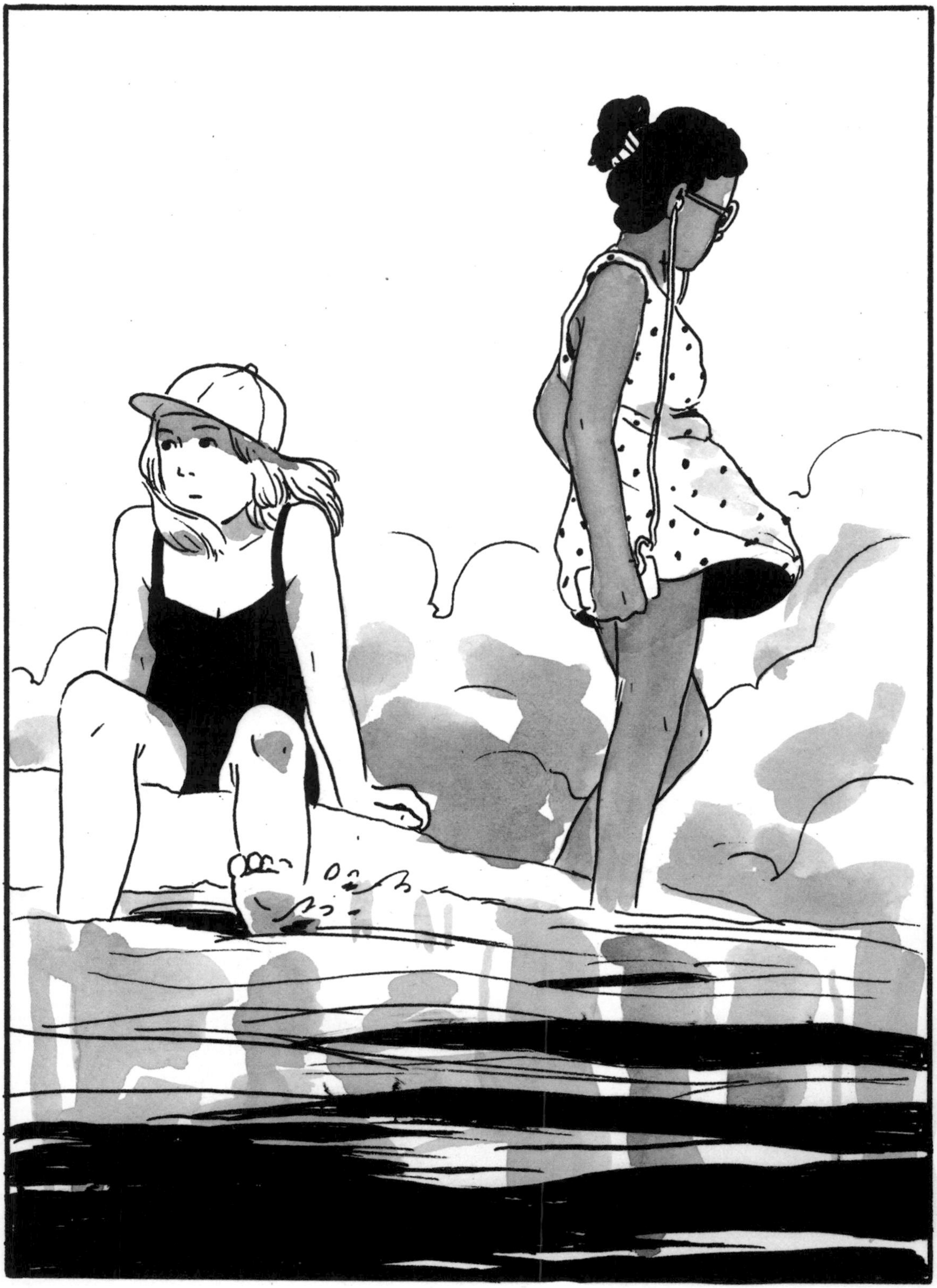

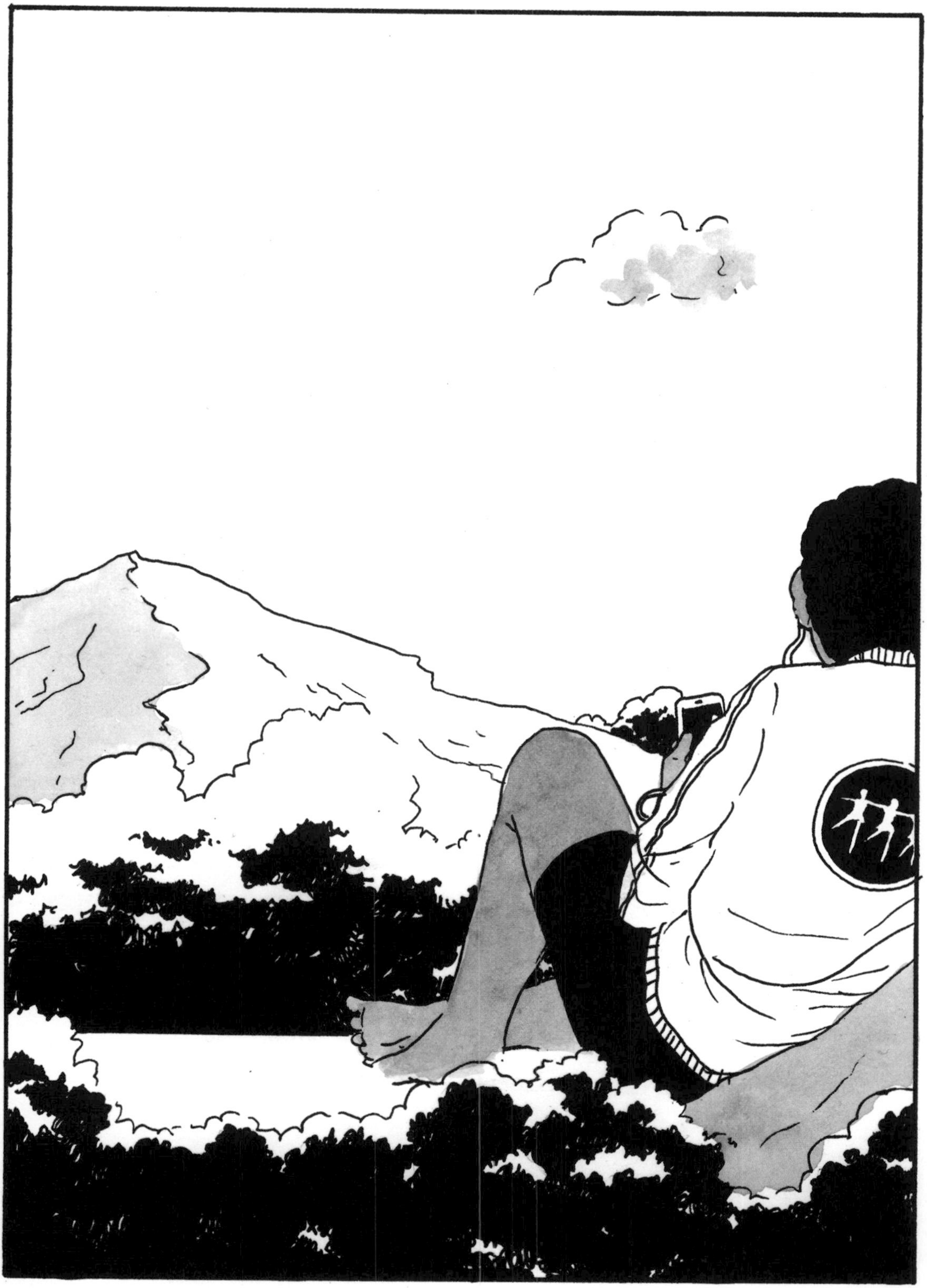

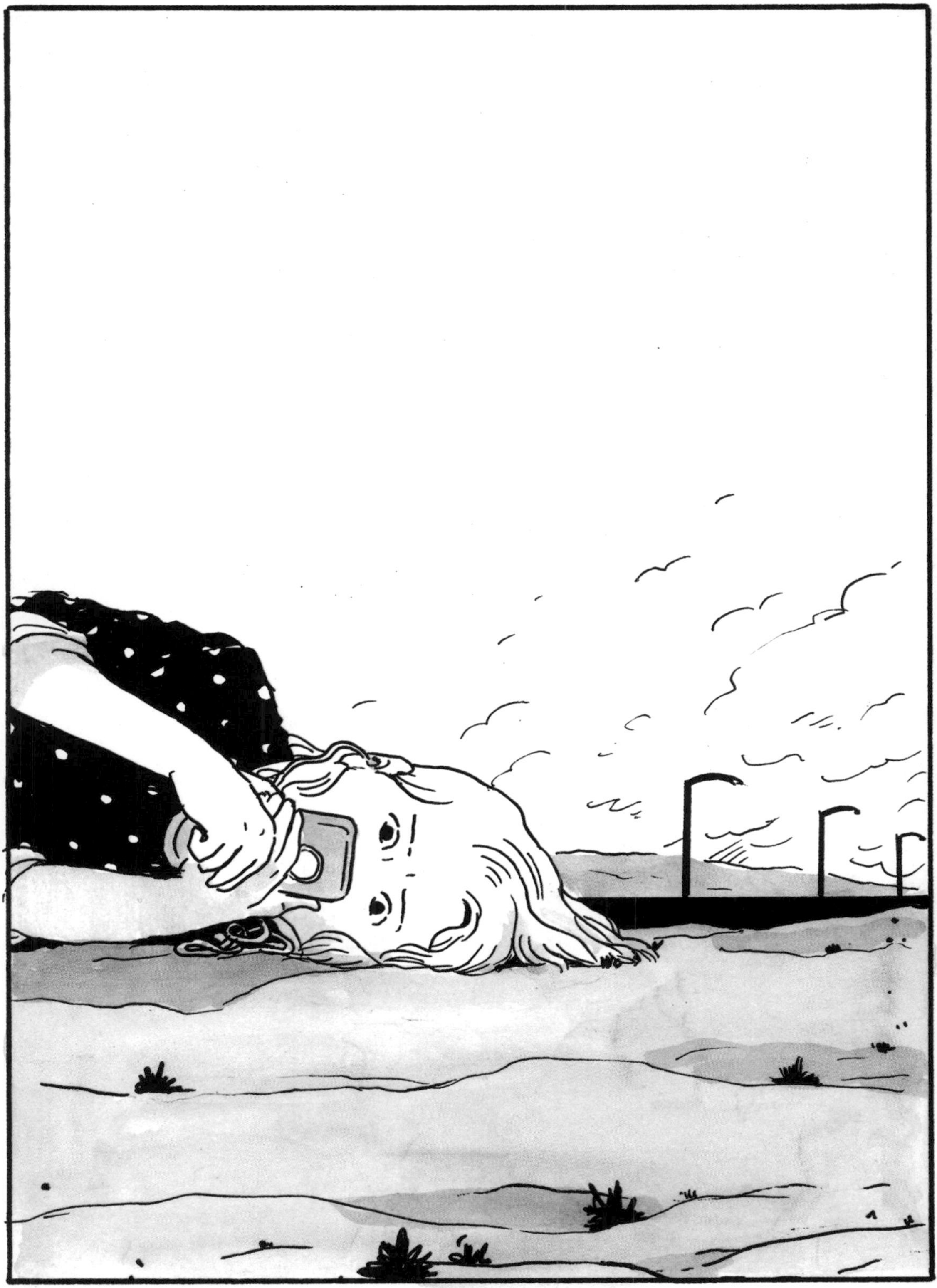

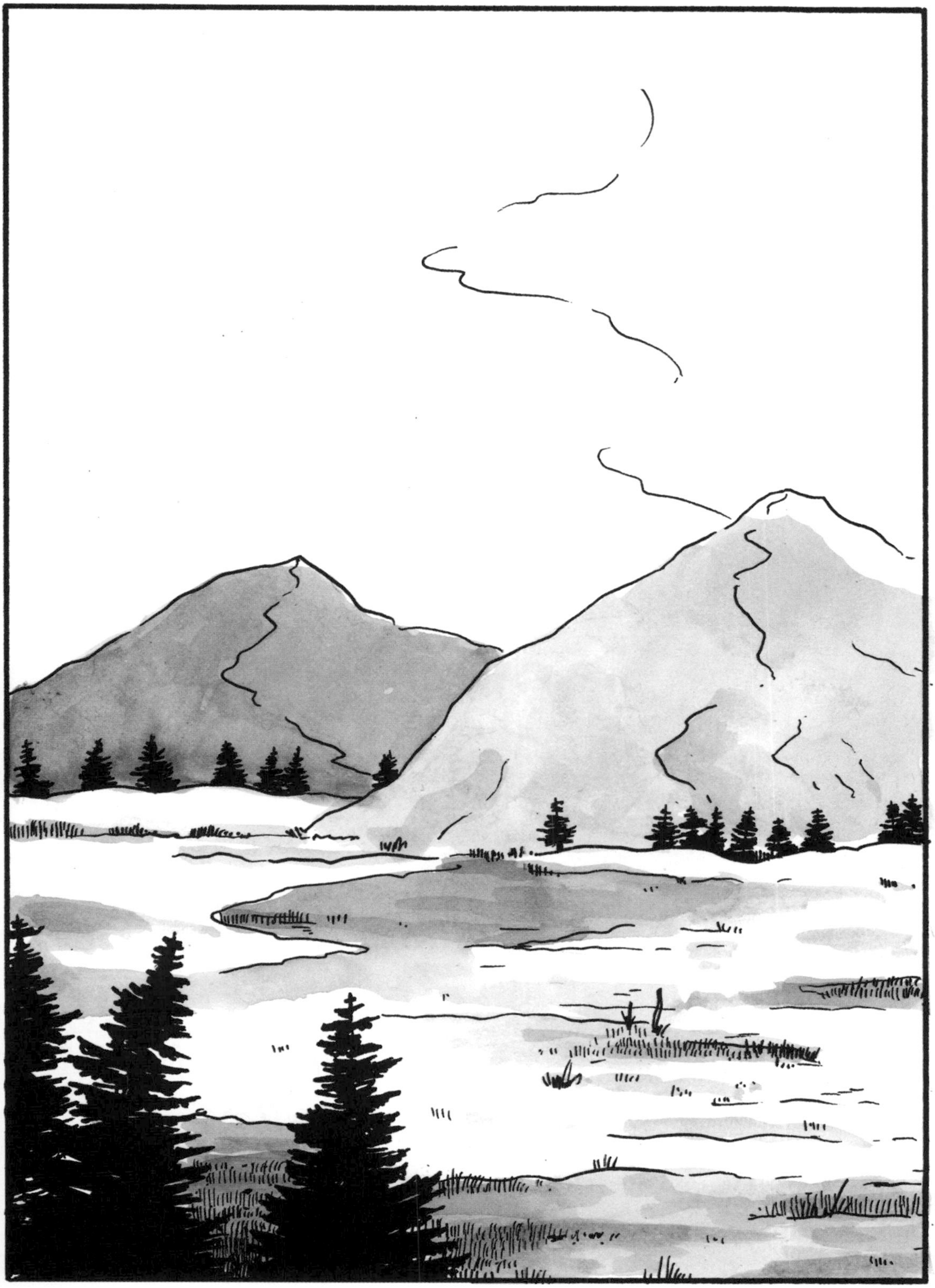

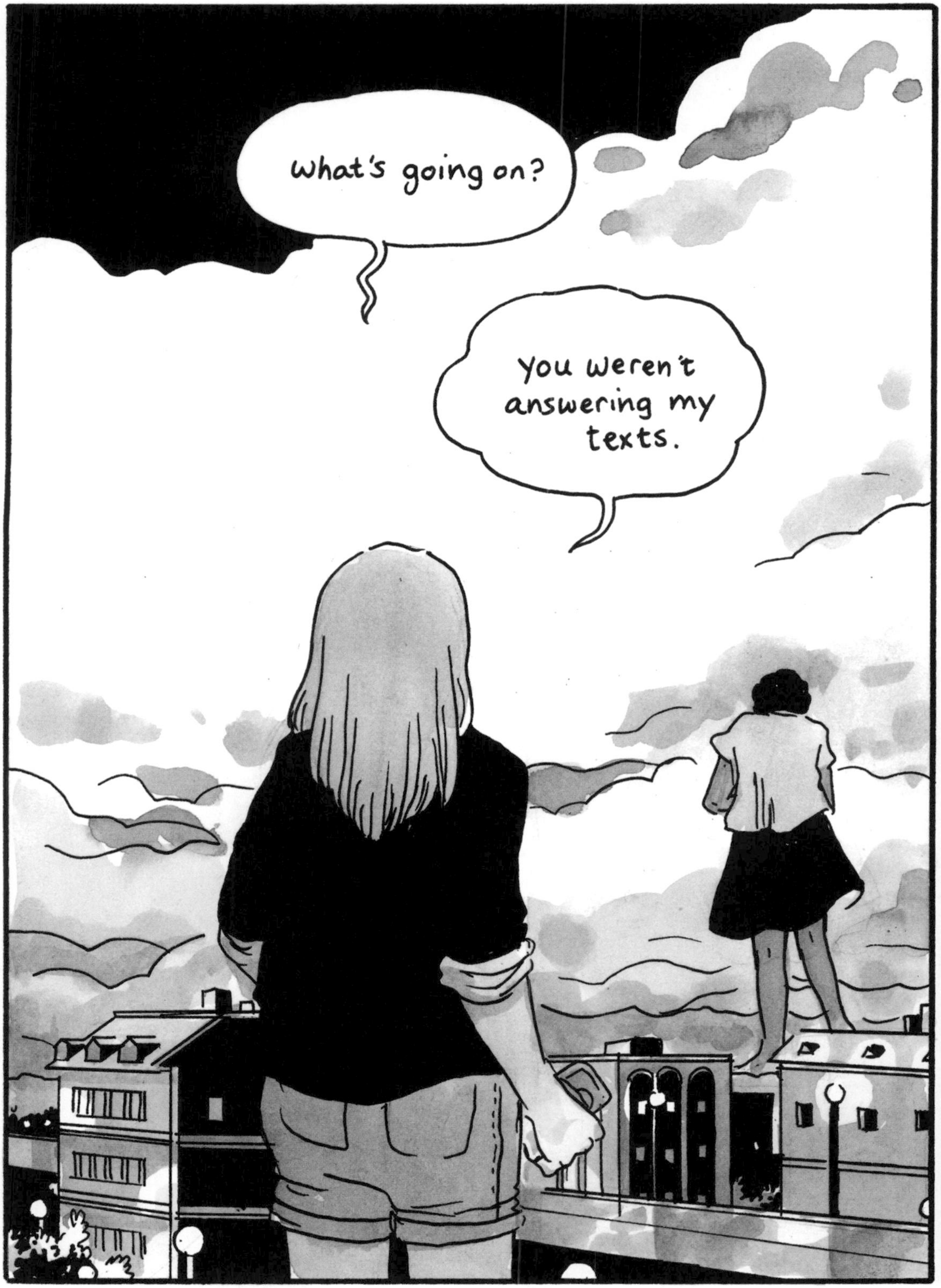
what's going on?
you weren't answering my texts.

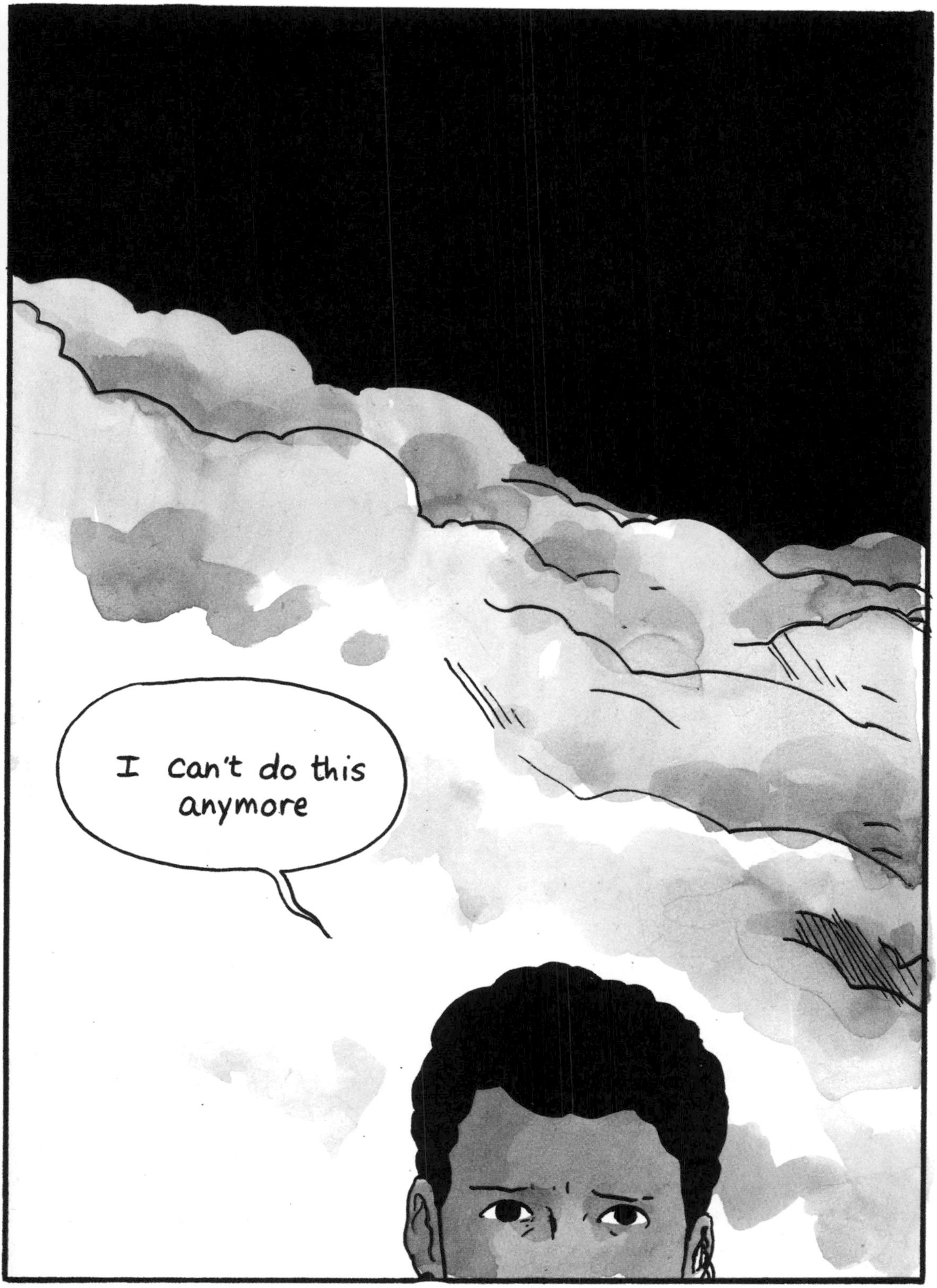
I can't do this anymore

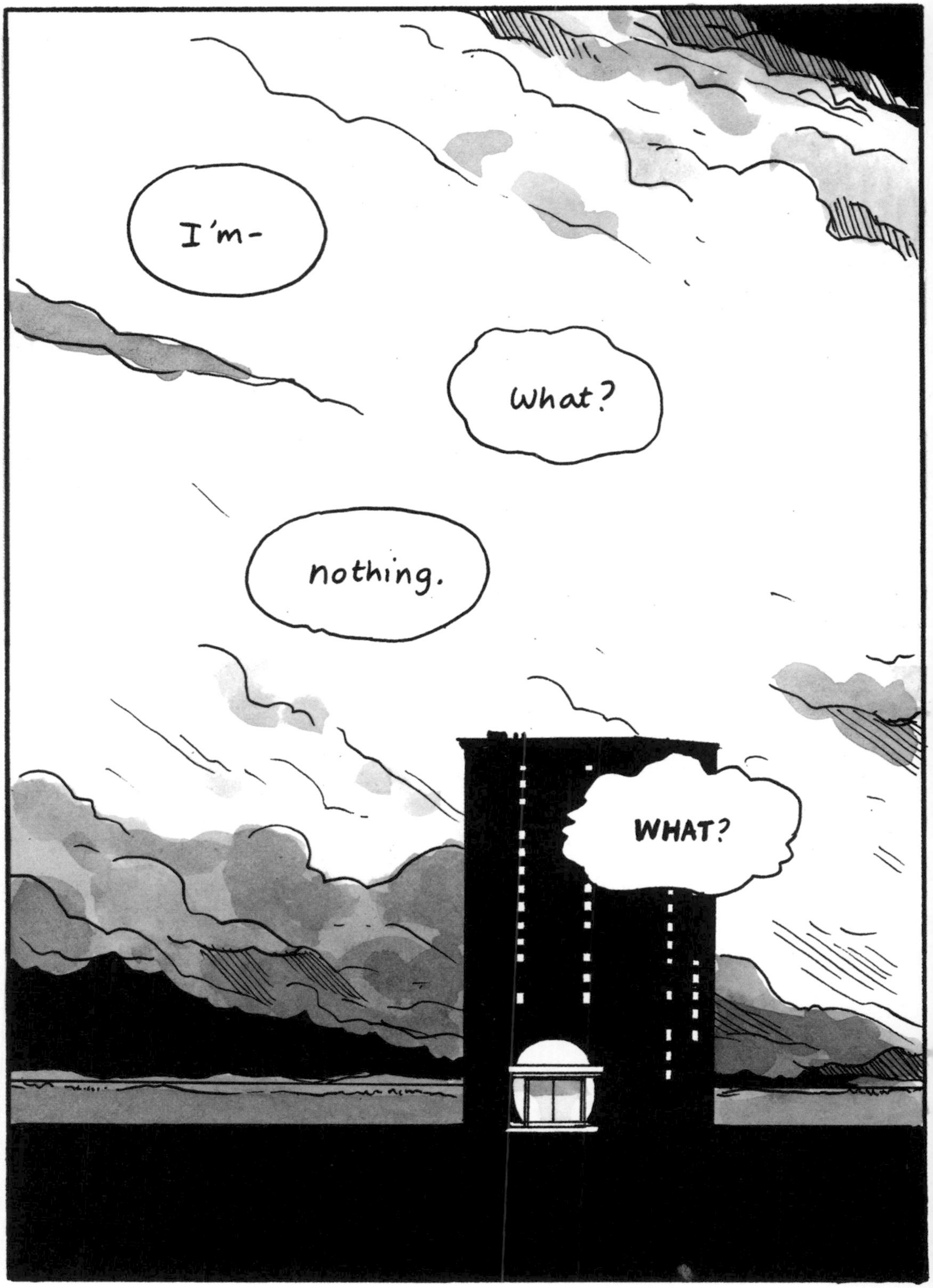
I'm-
What?
nothing.
WHAT?

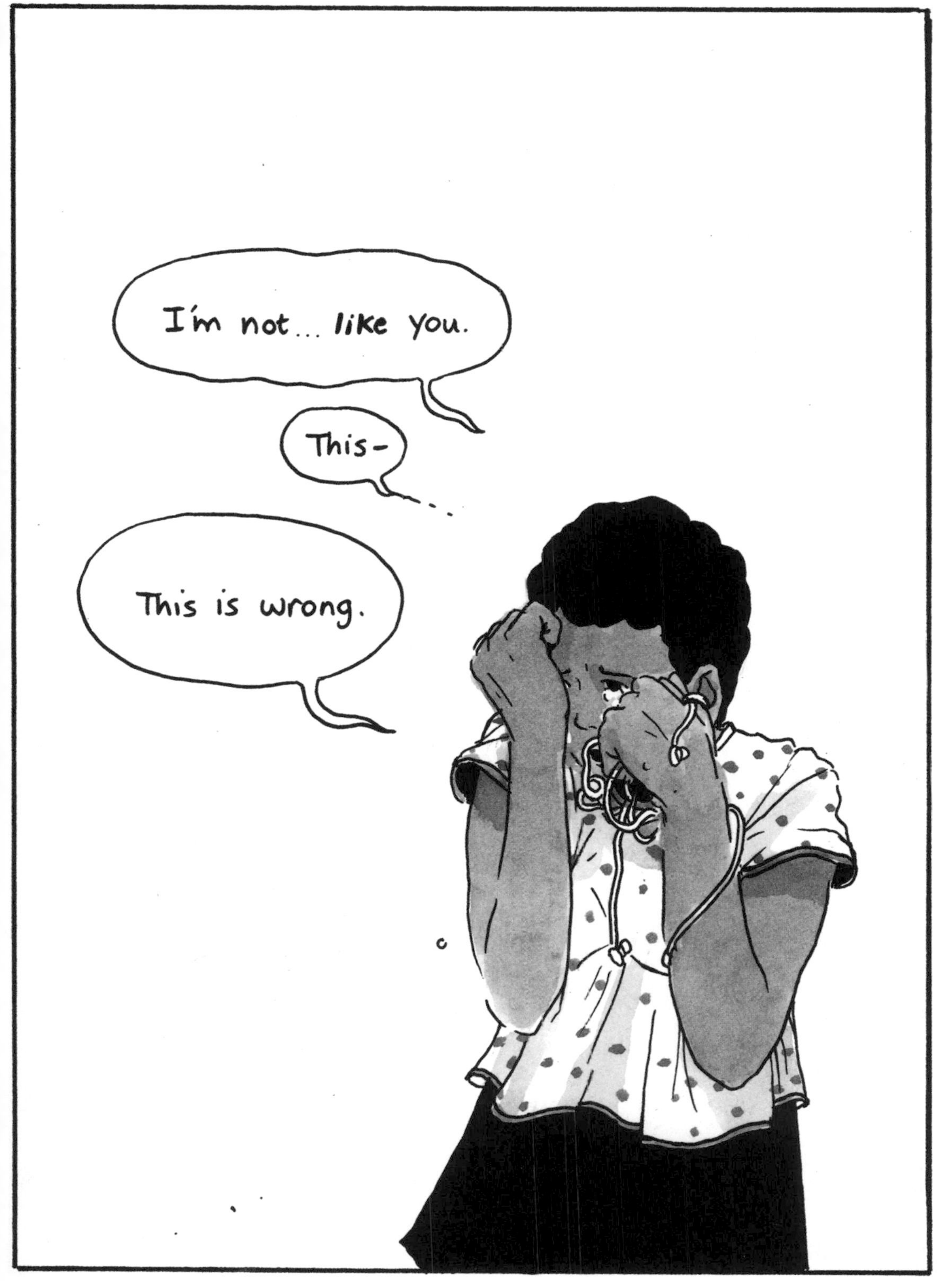
I'm not... like you.
This-
This is wrong.

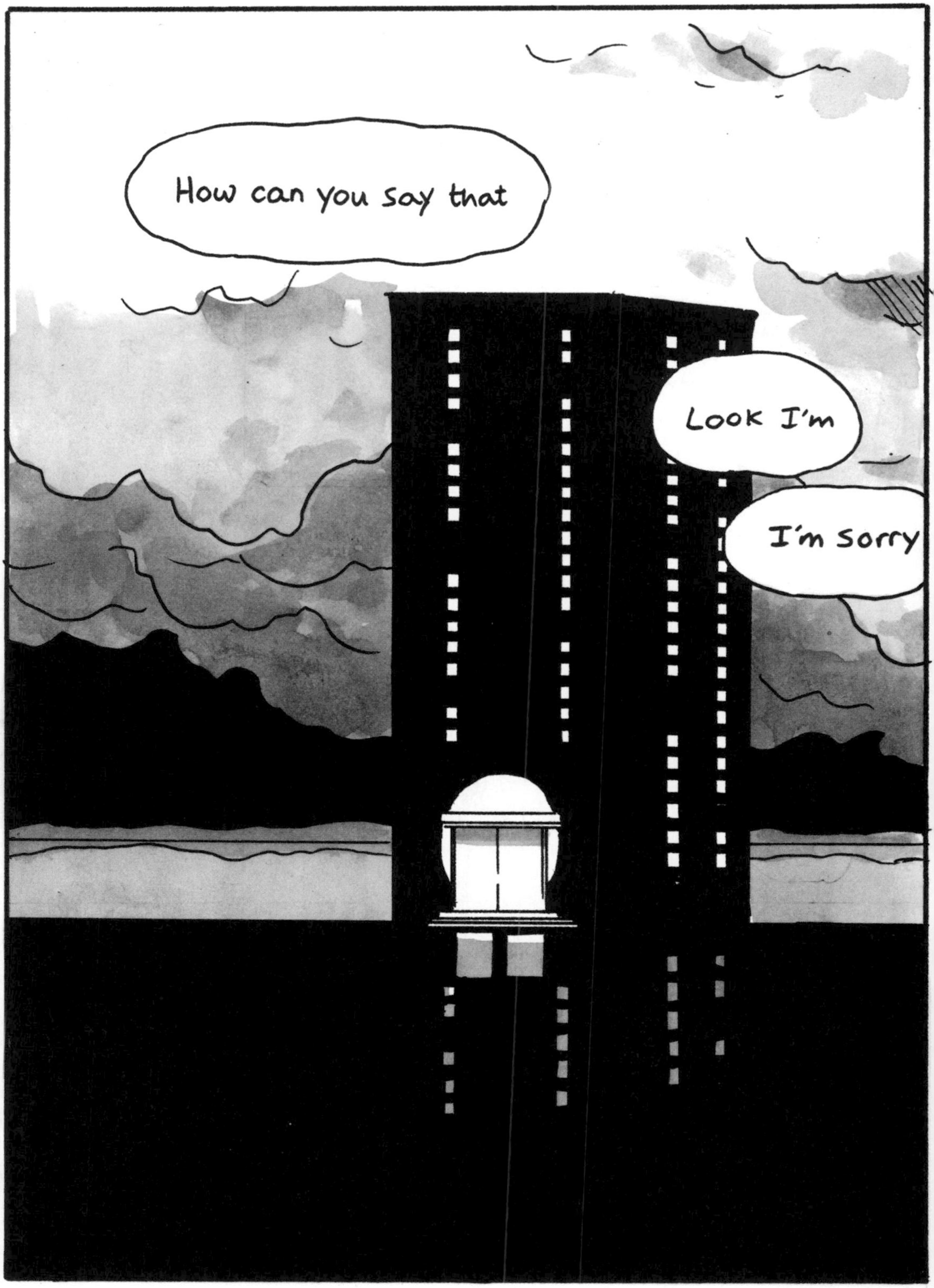
How can you say that
Look I'm
I'm sorry

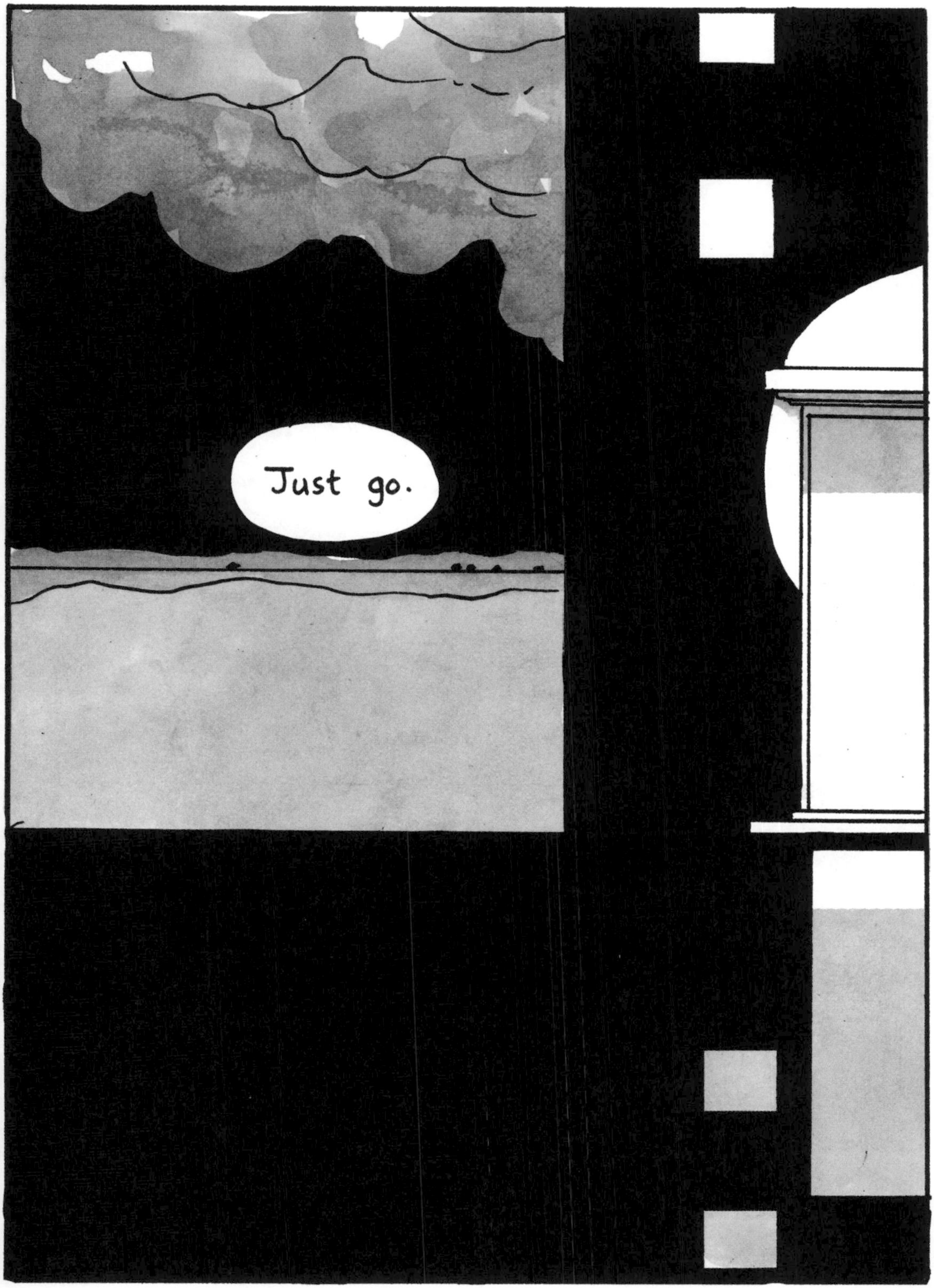
Just go.

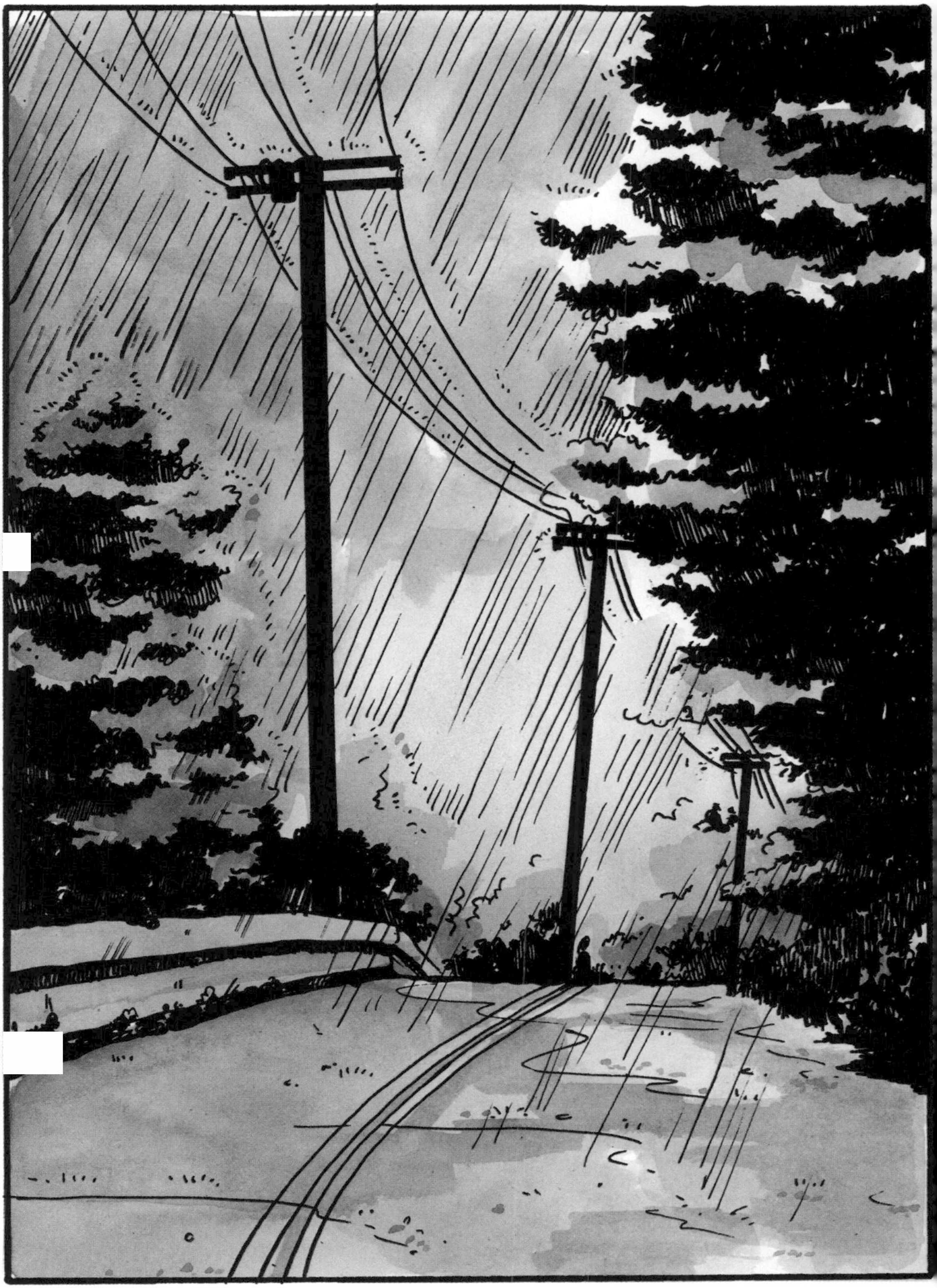

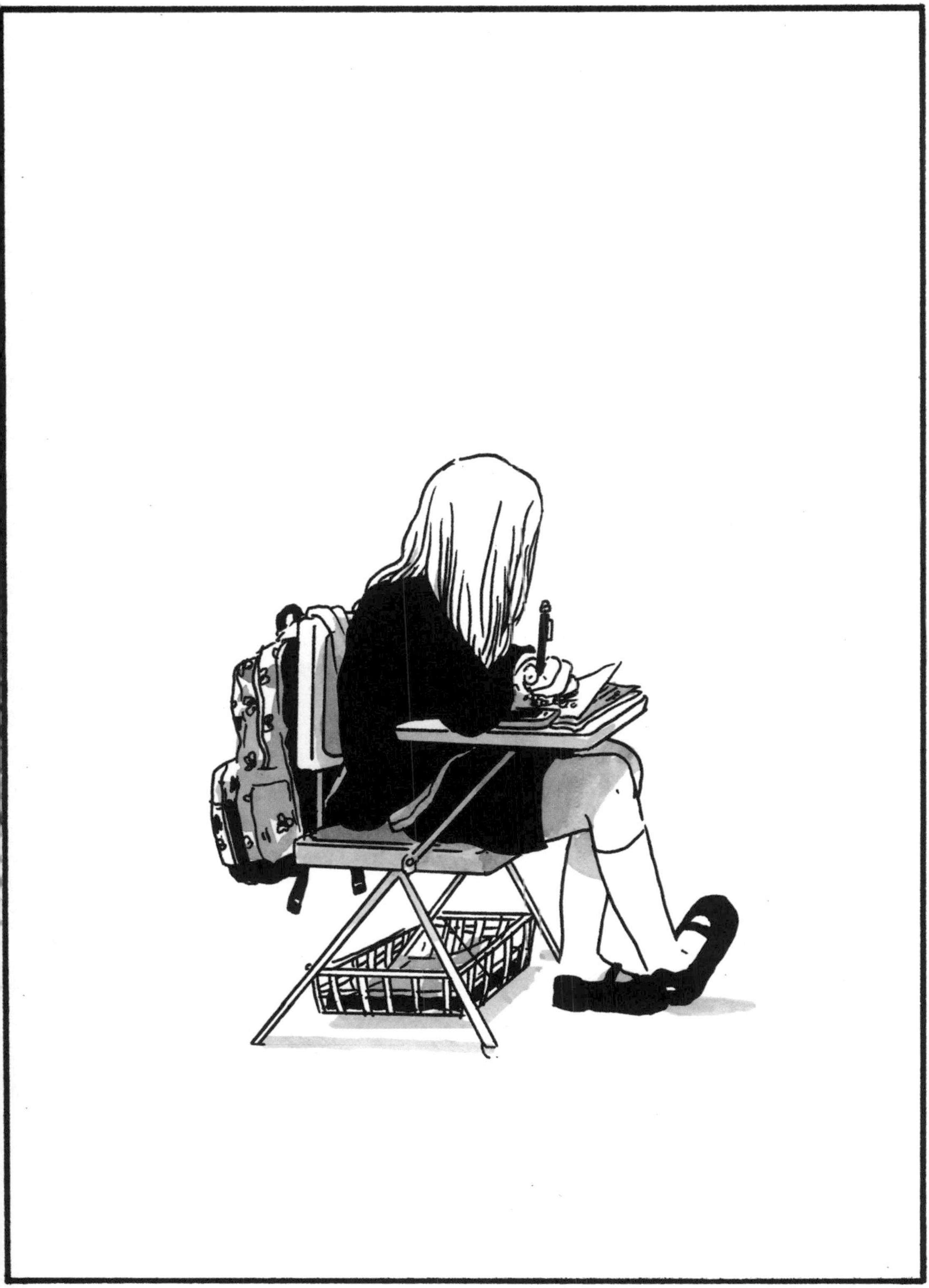

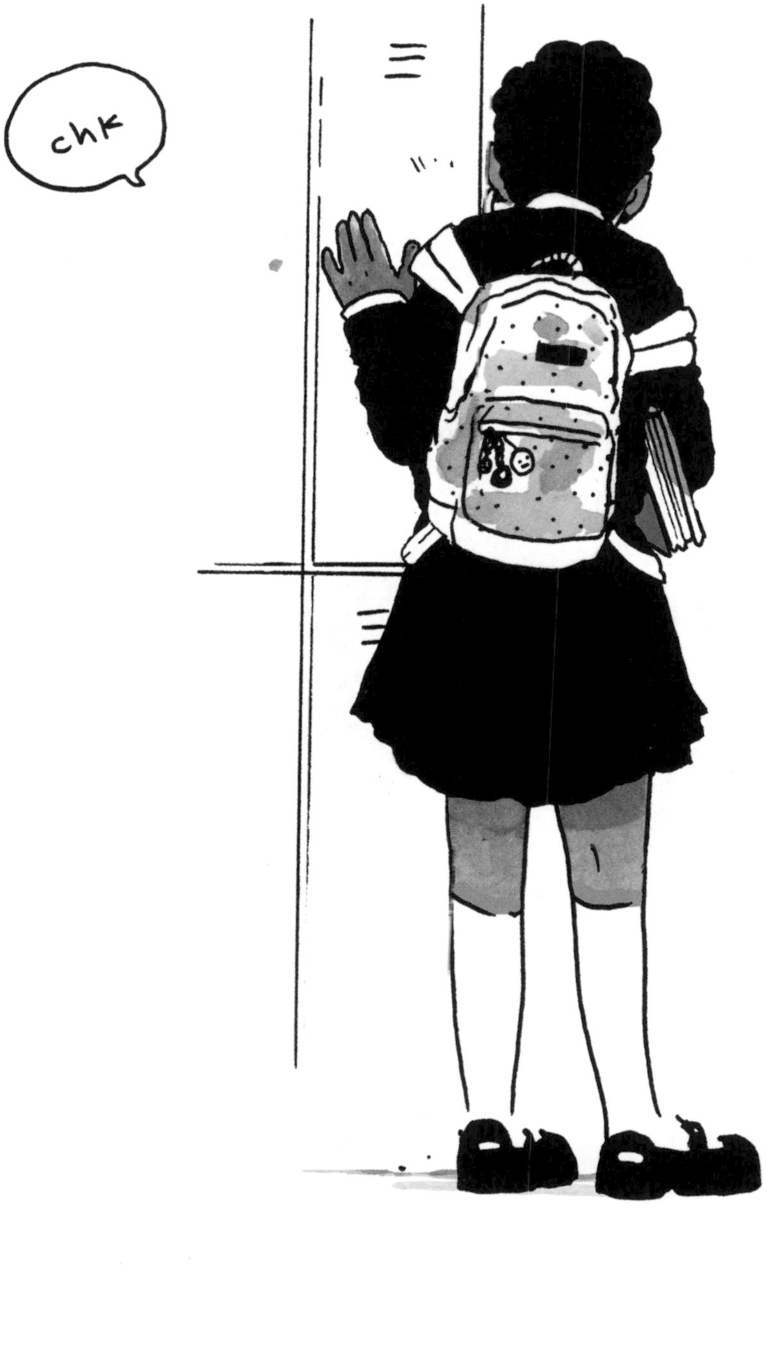
chk

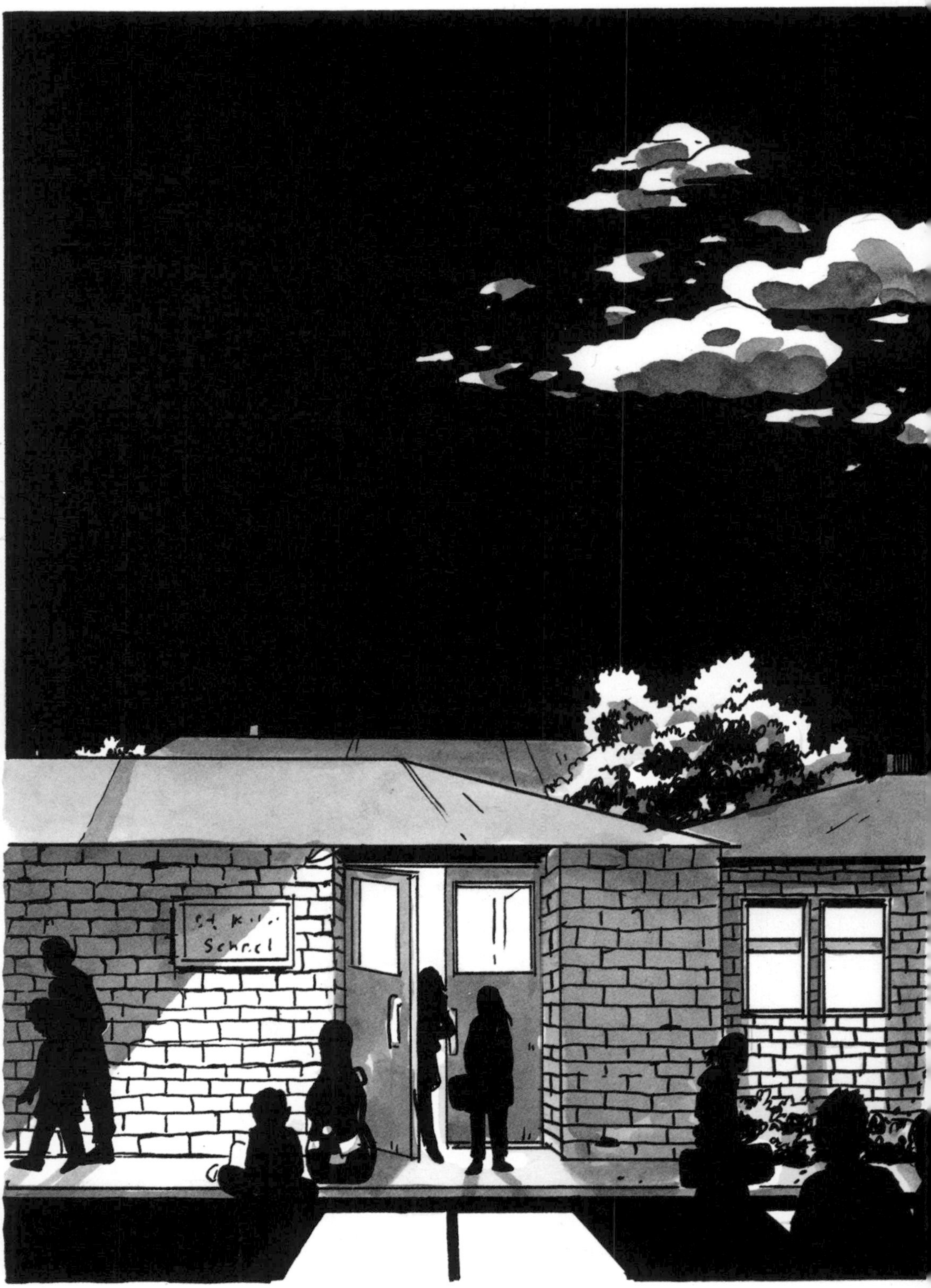

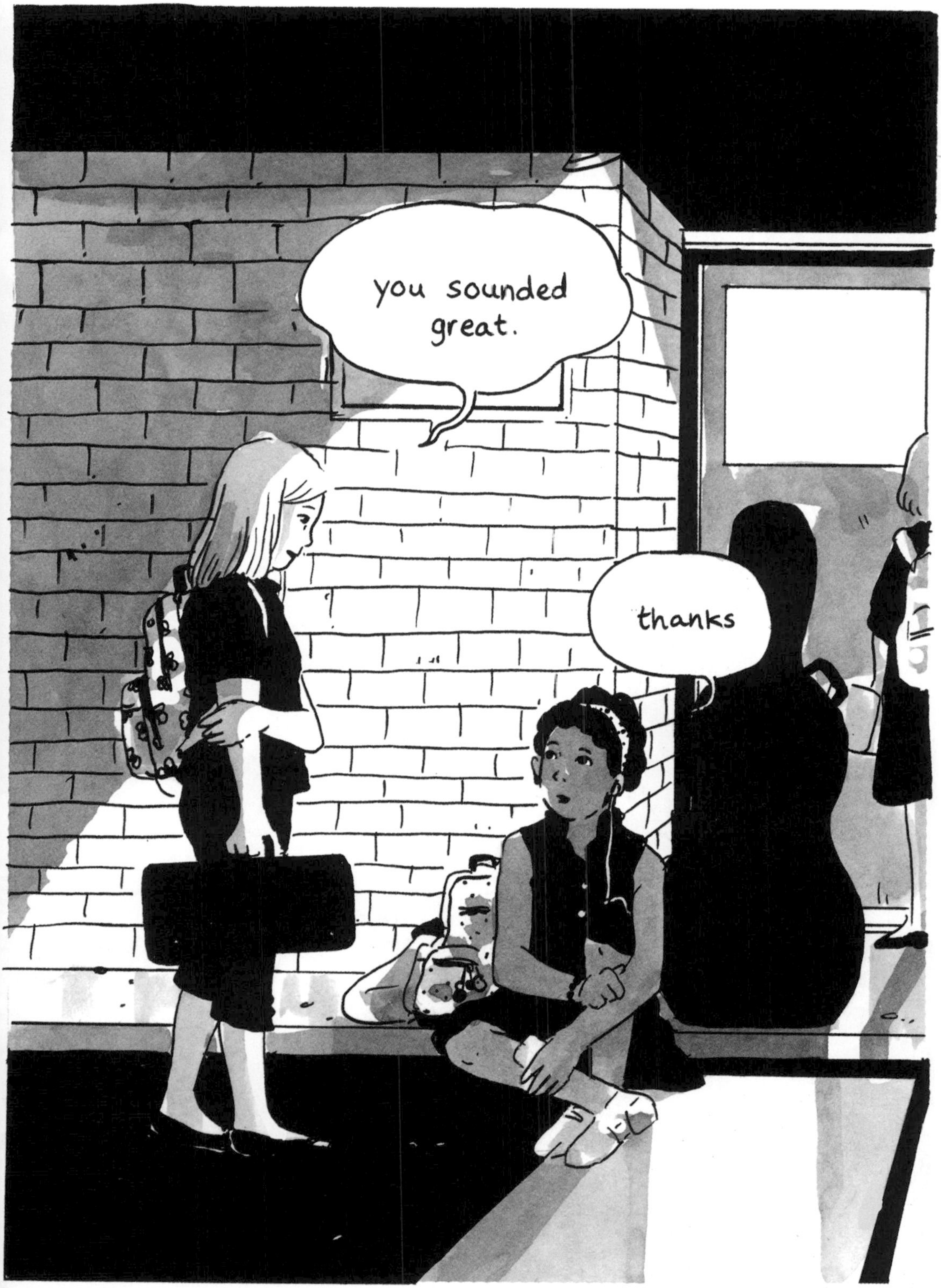
you sounded great.
thanks

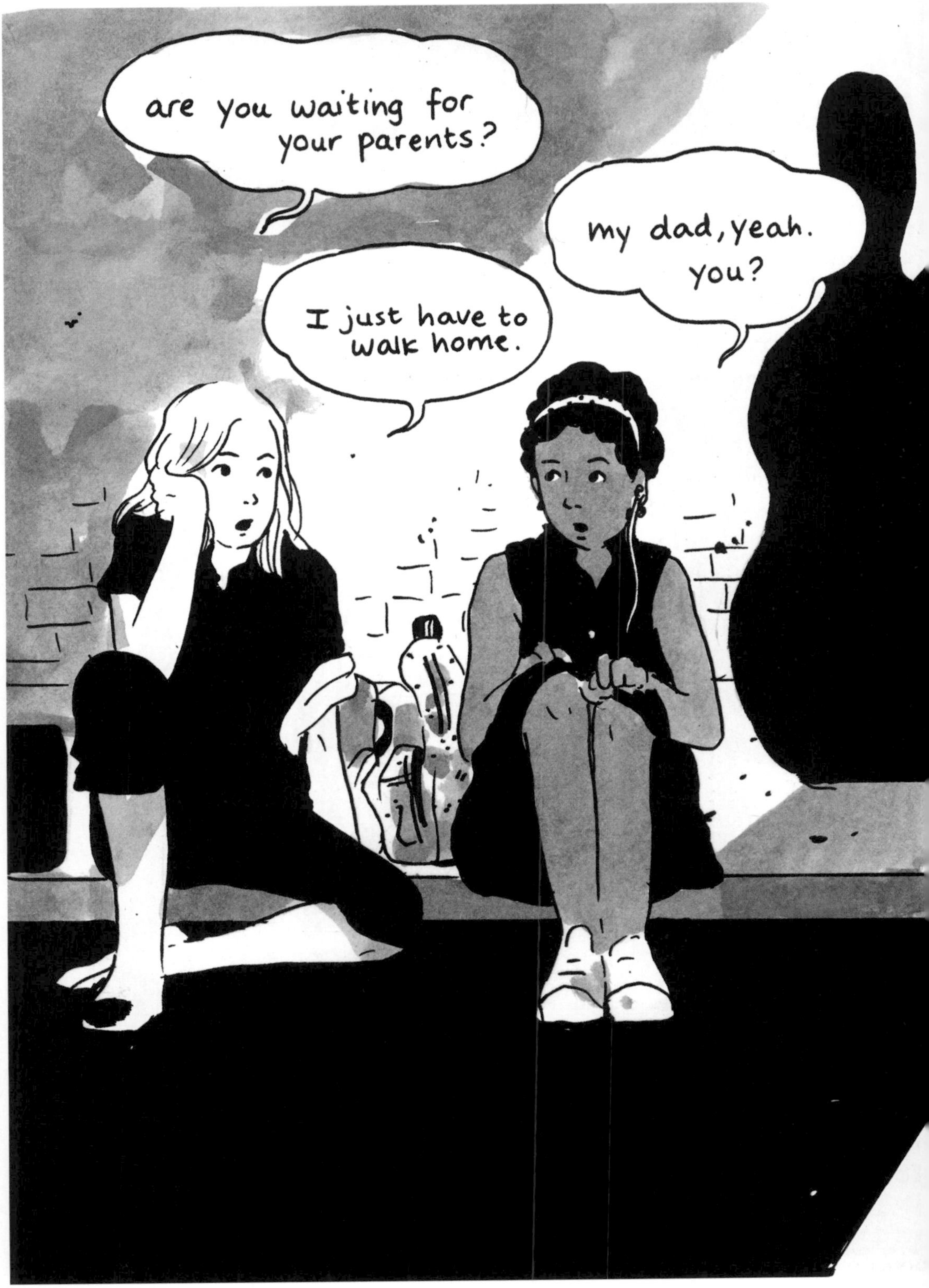
are you waiting for your parents?
my dad, yeah. you?
I just have to walk home.

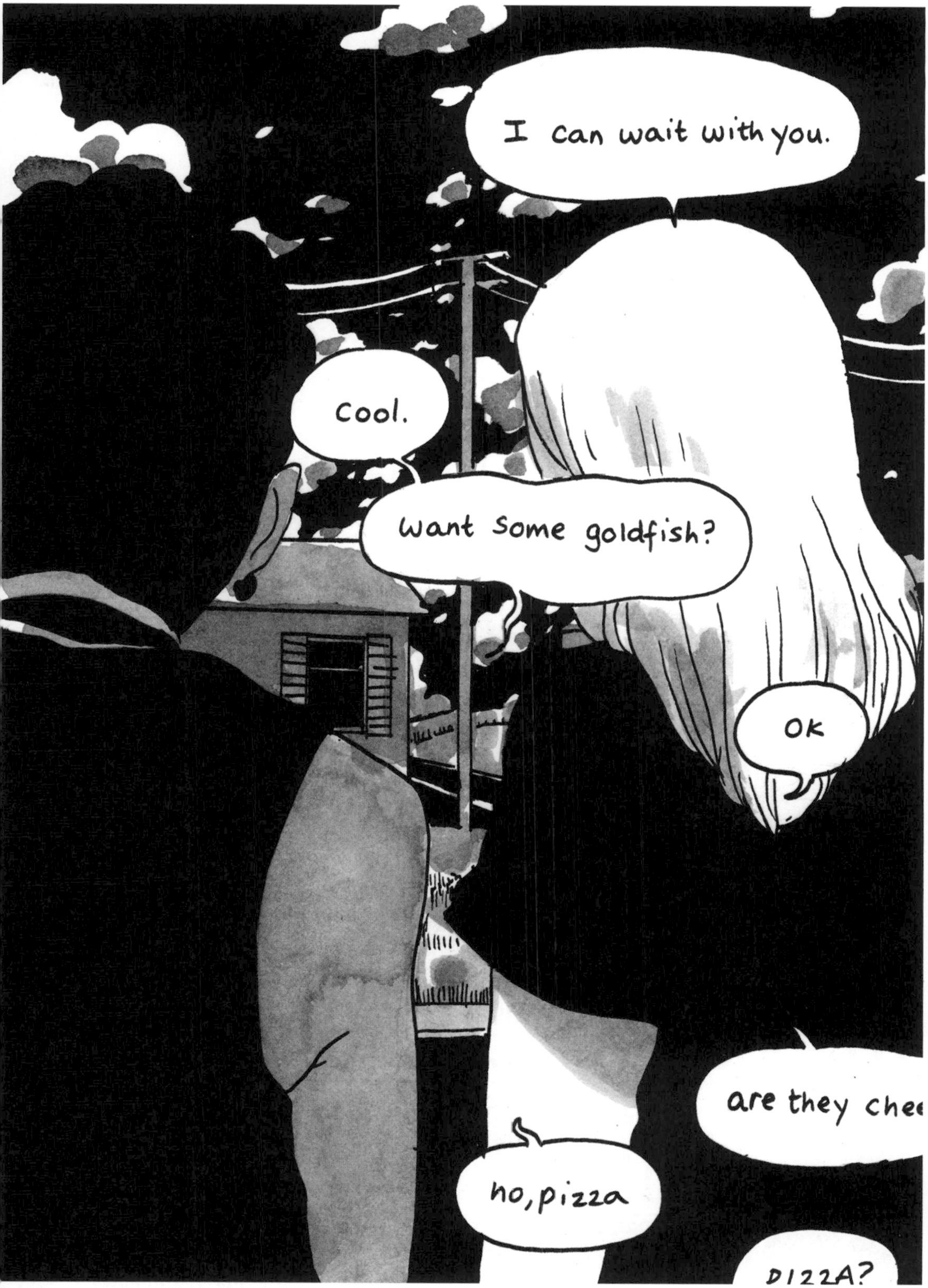
I can wait with you.
Cool.
Want some goldfish?
ok
are they chee
no, pizza
PIZZA?

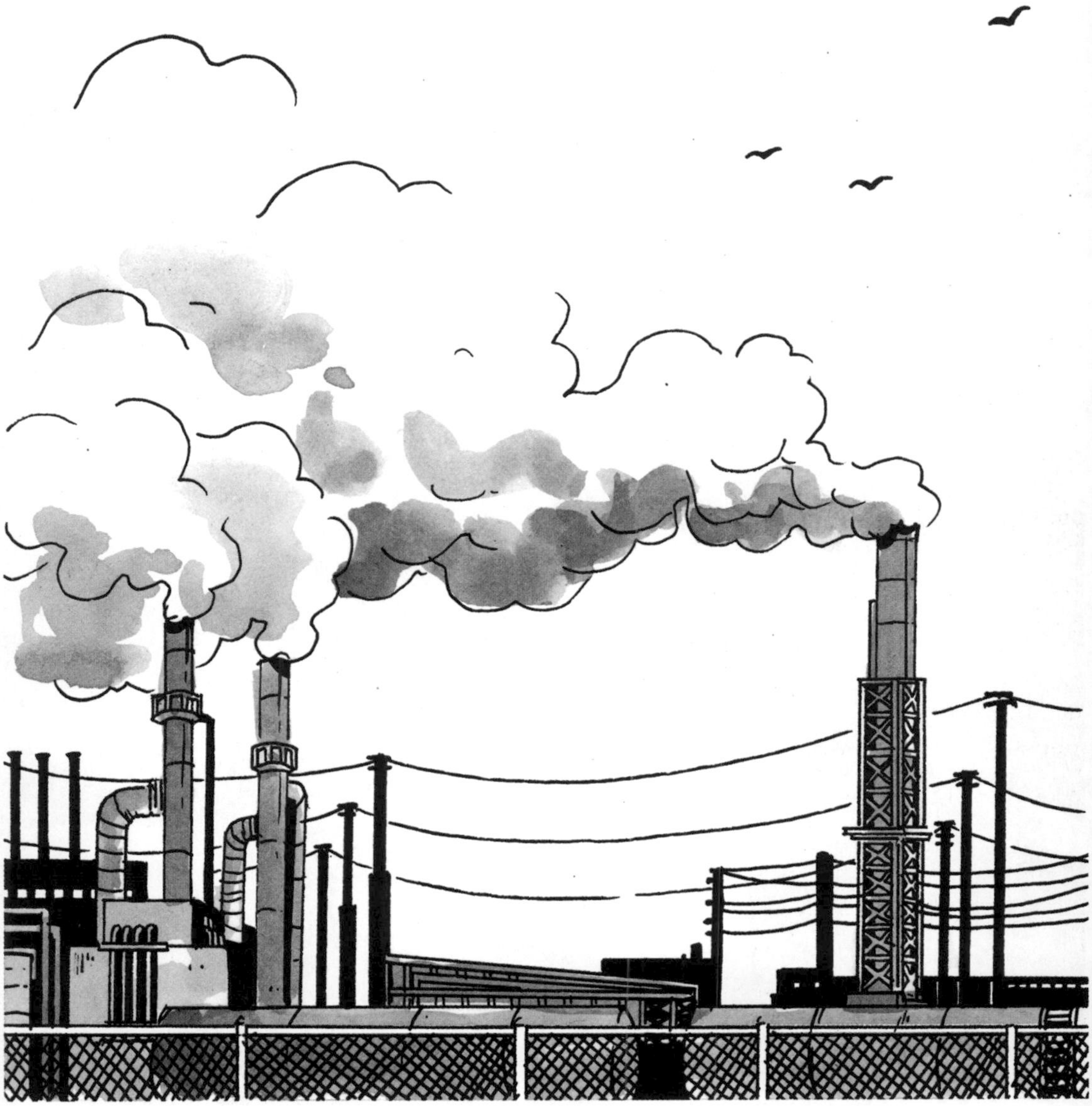

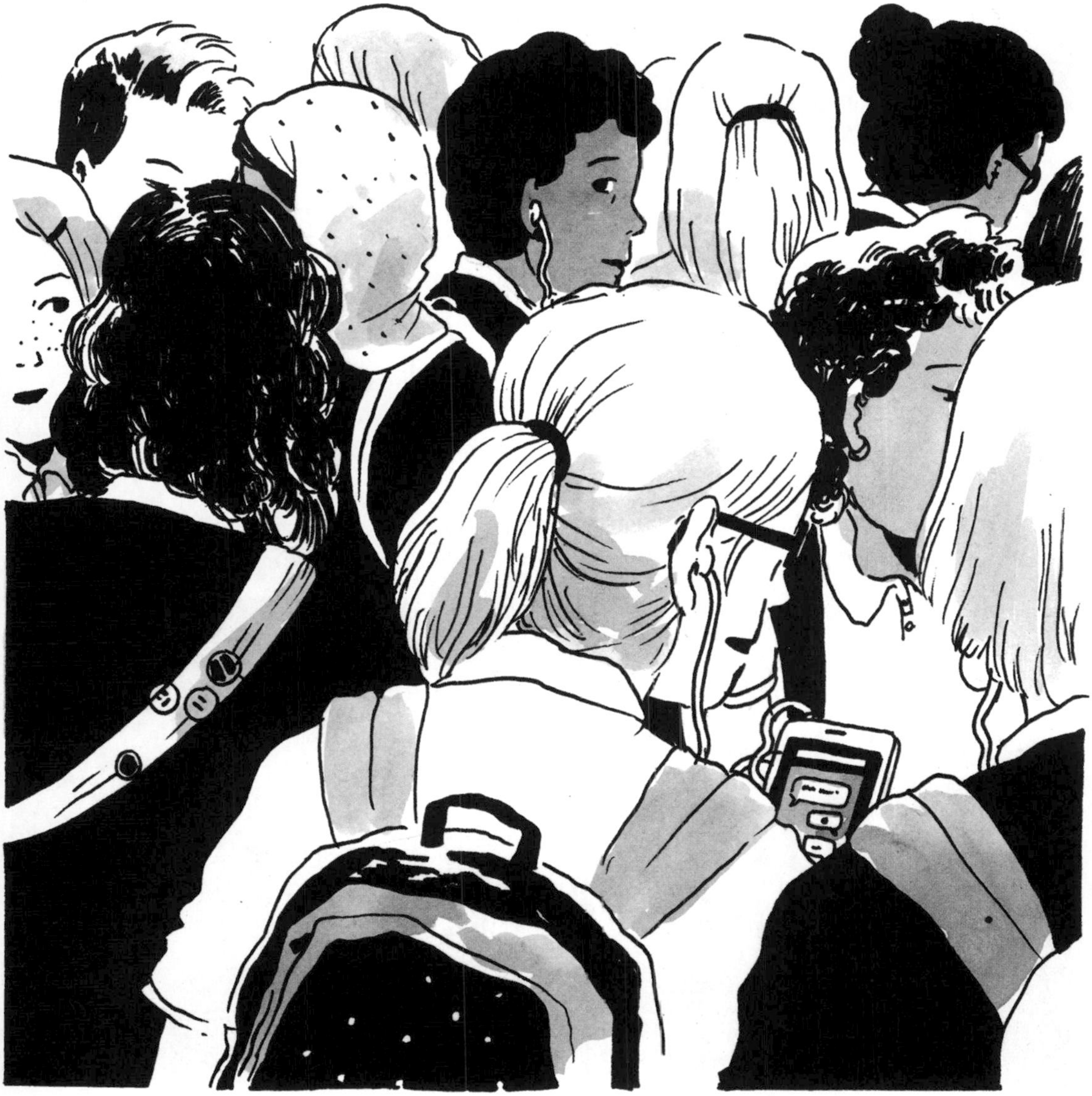

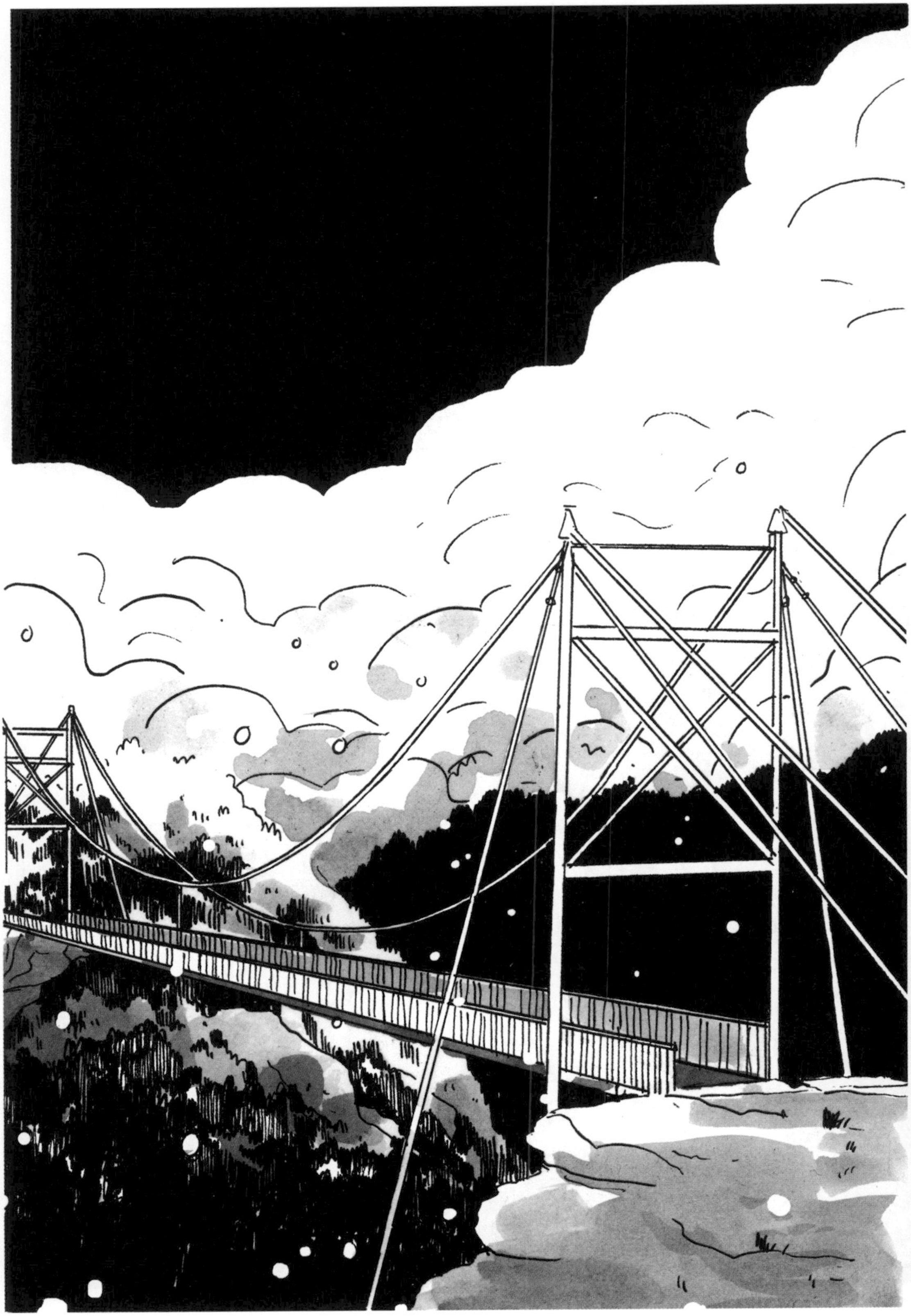

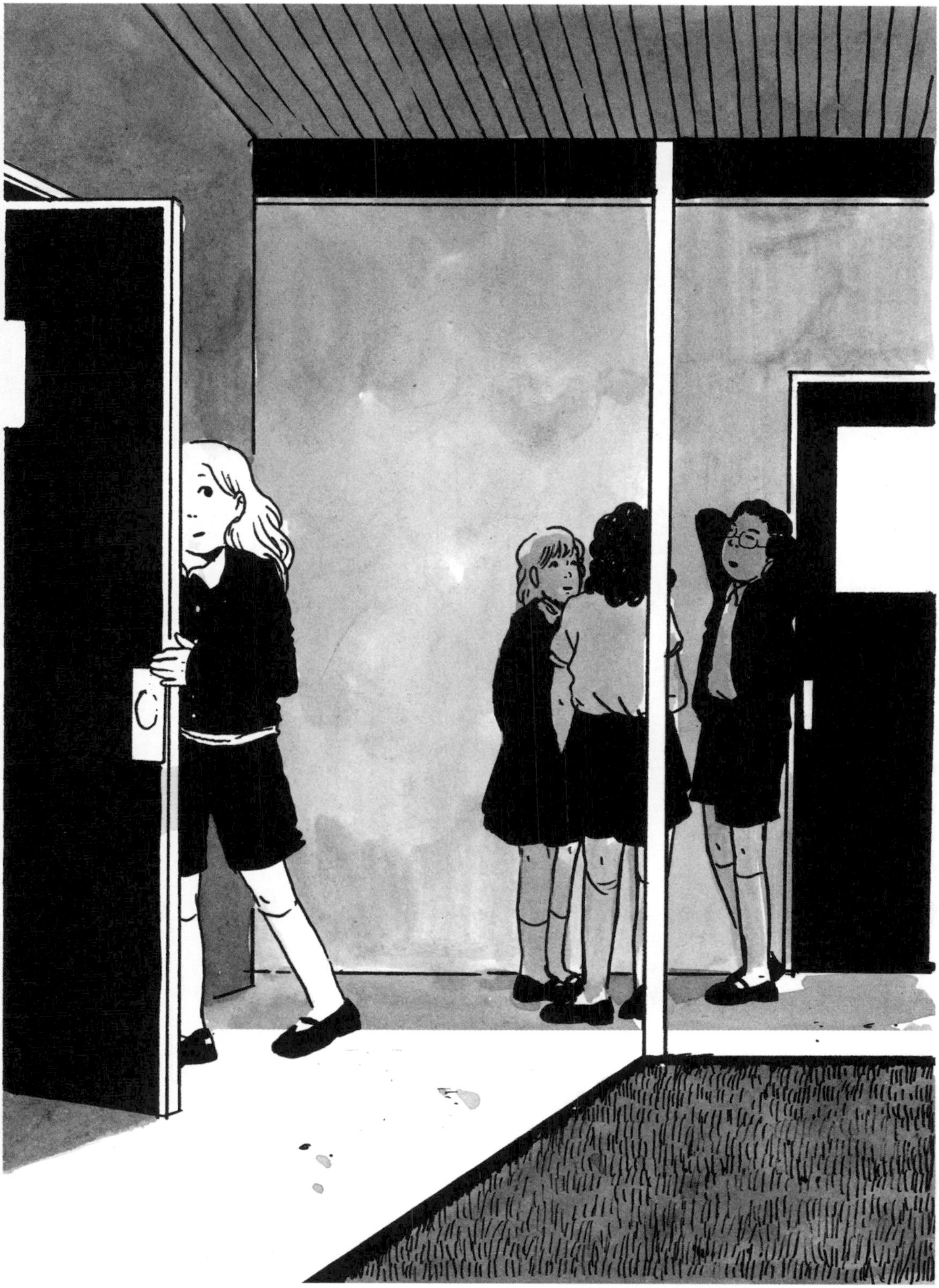

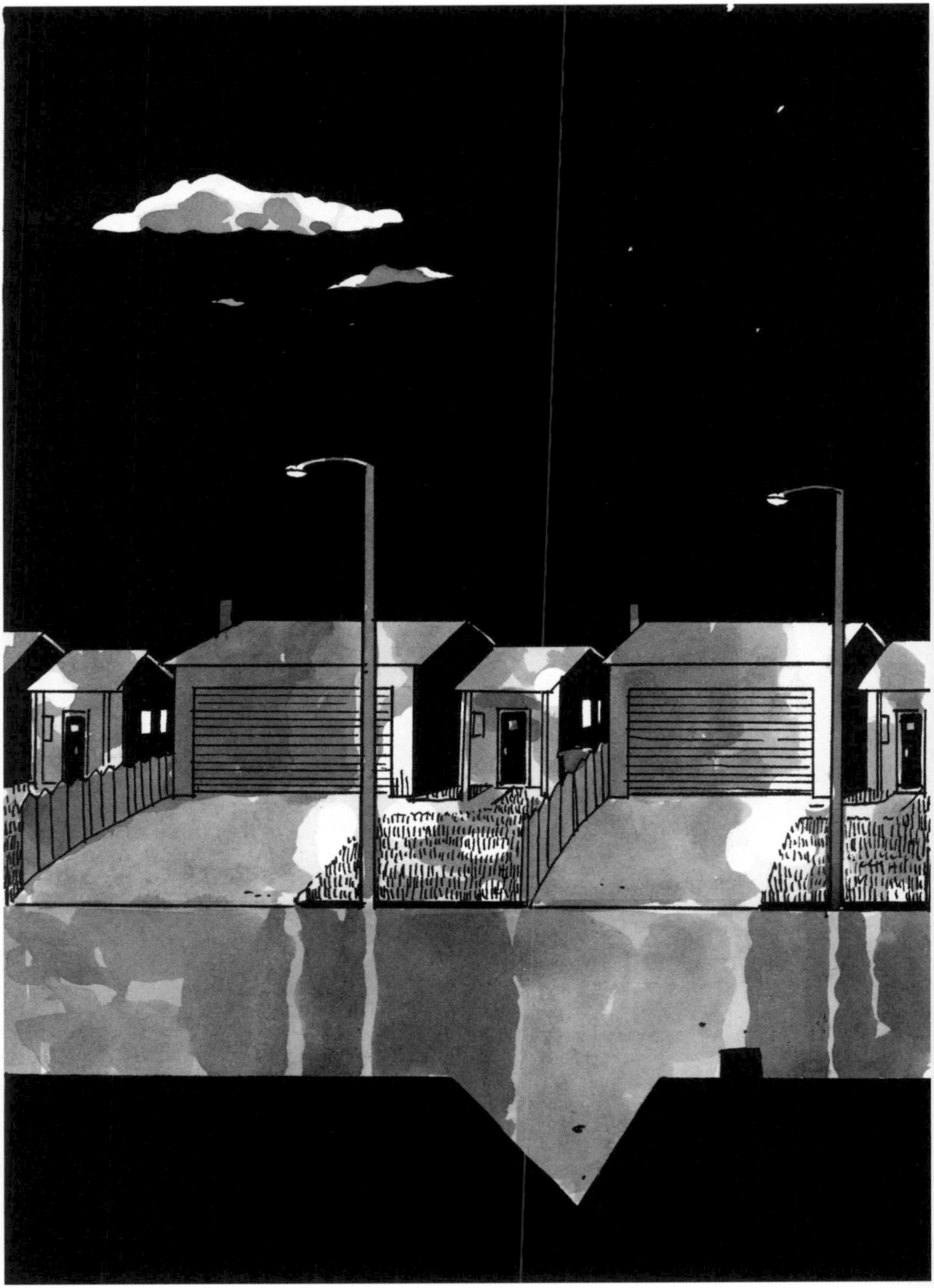

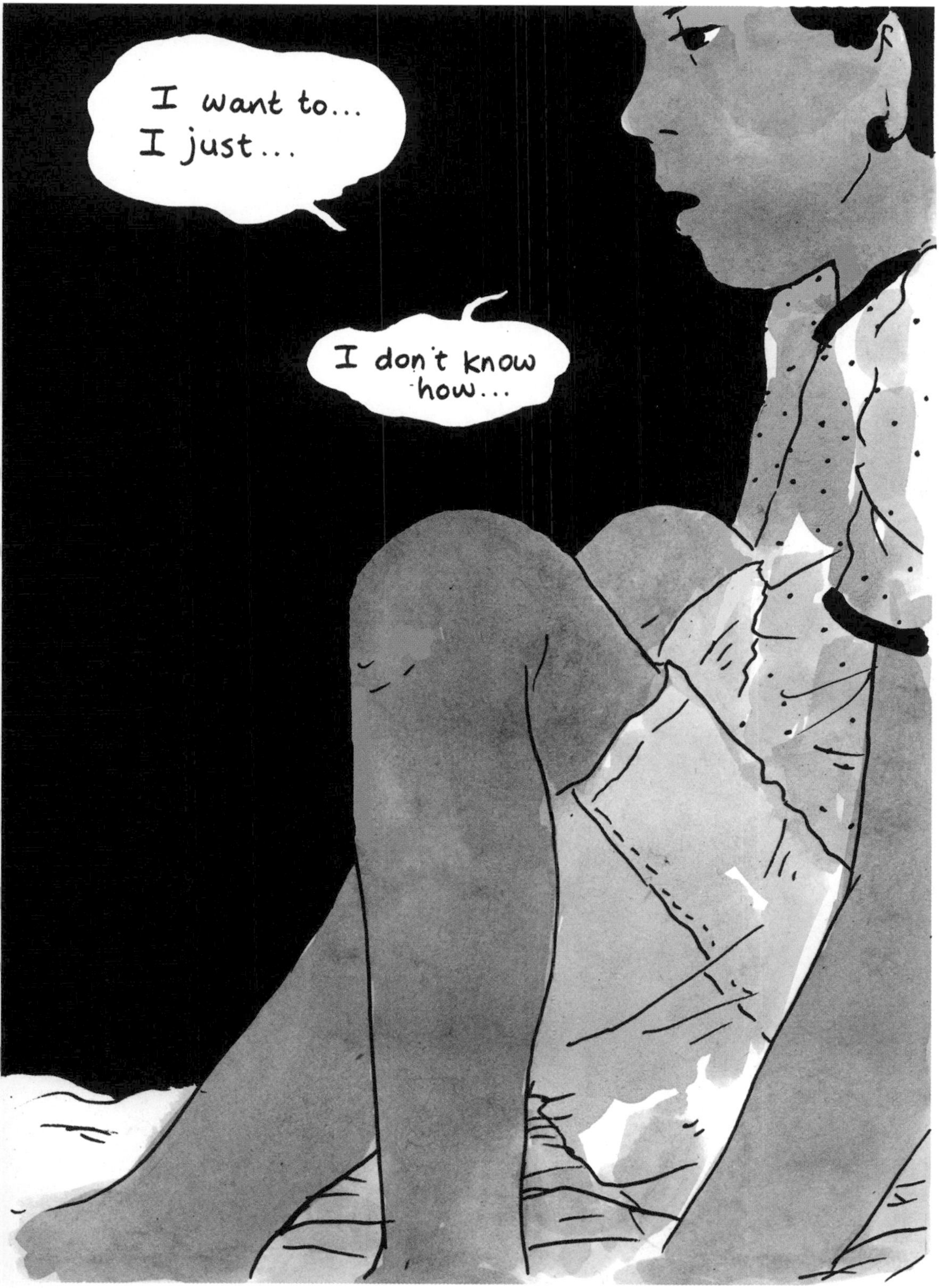
I want to...
I just...
I don't know how...

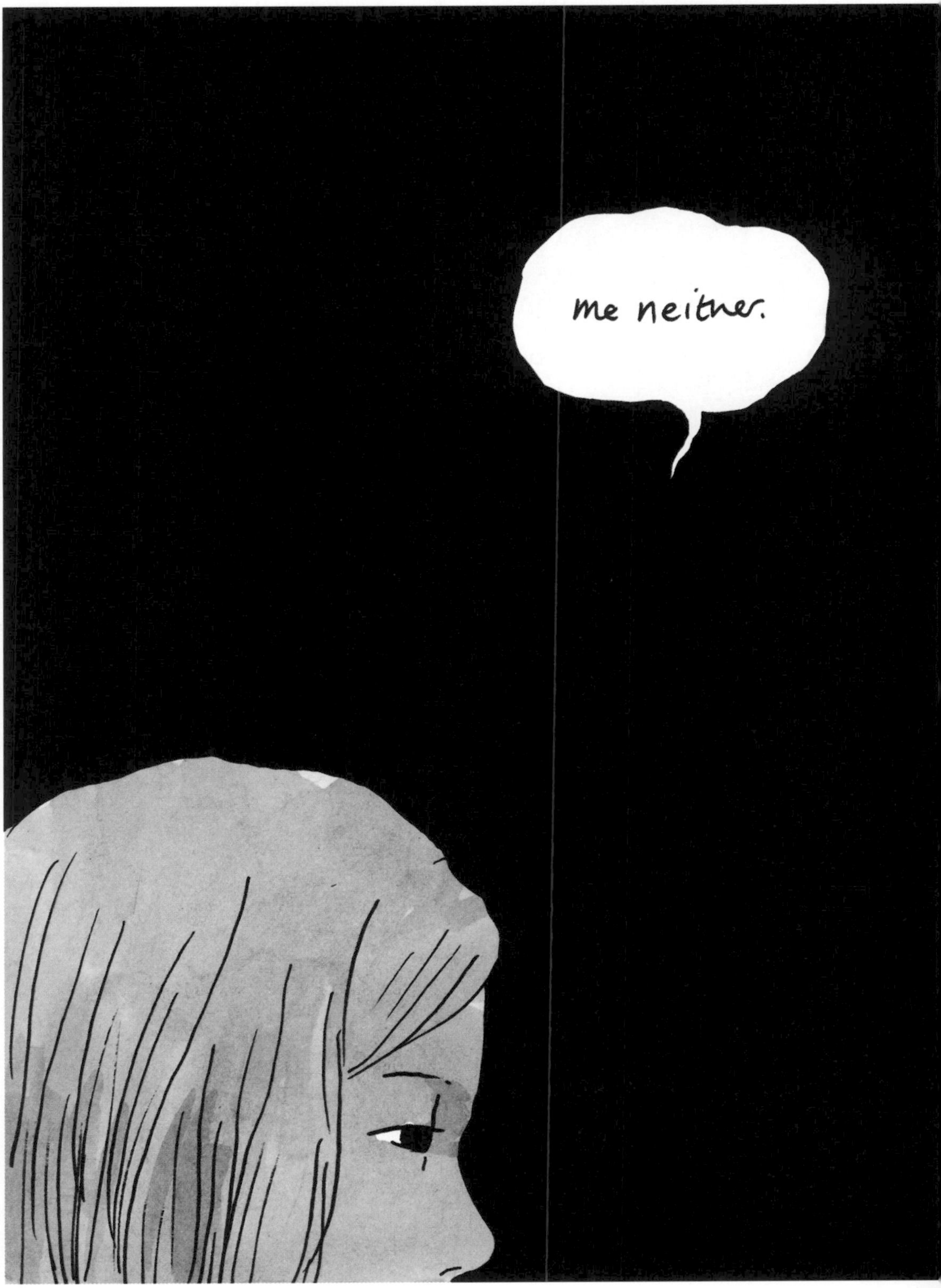
me neither.

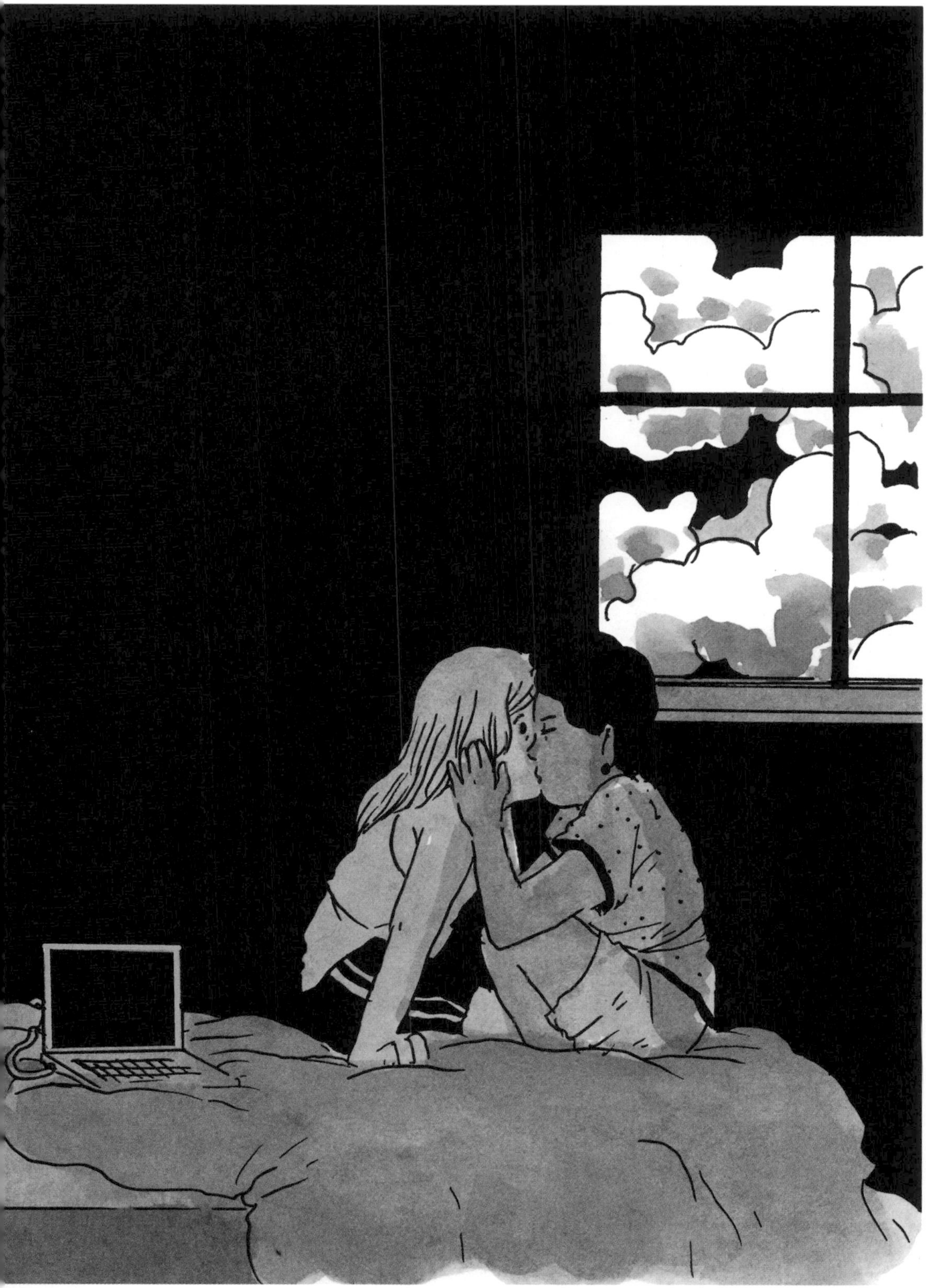

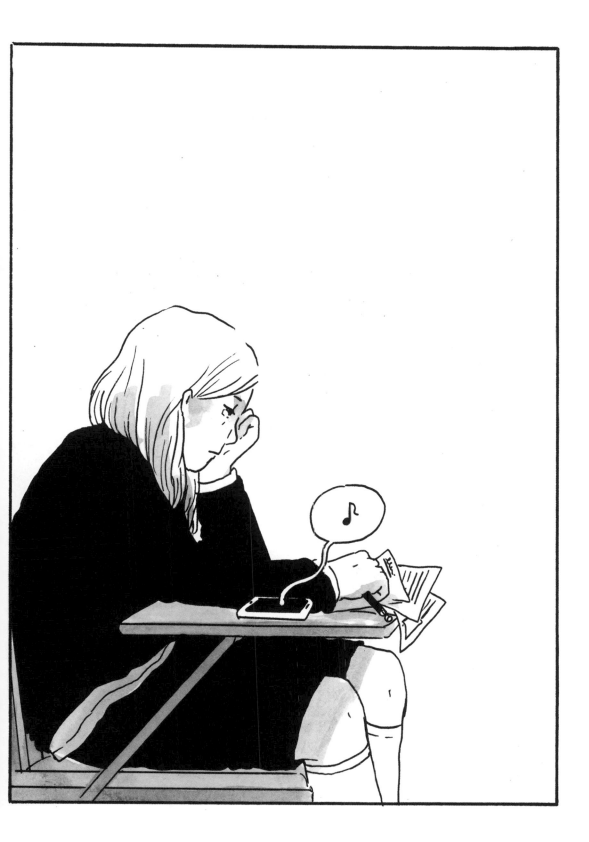

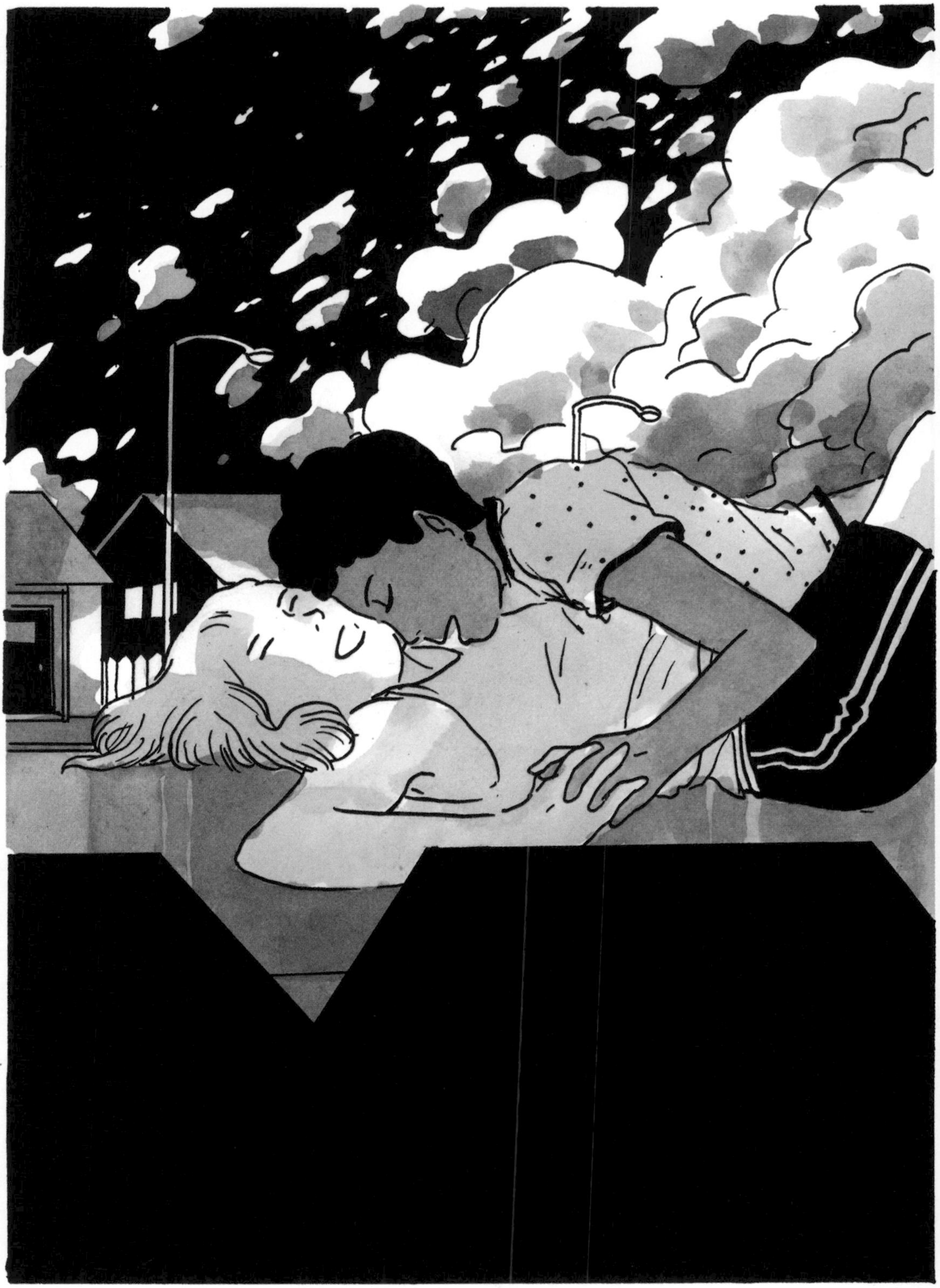

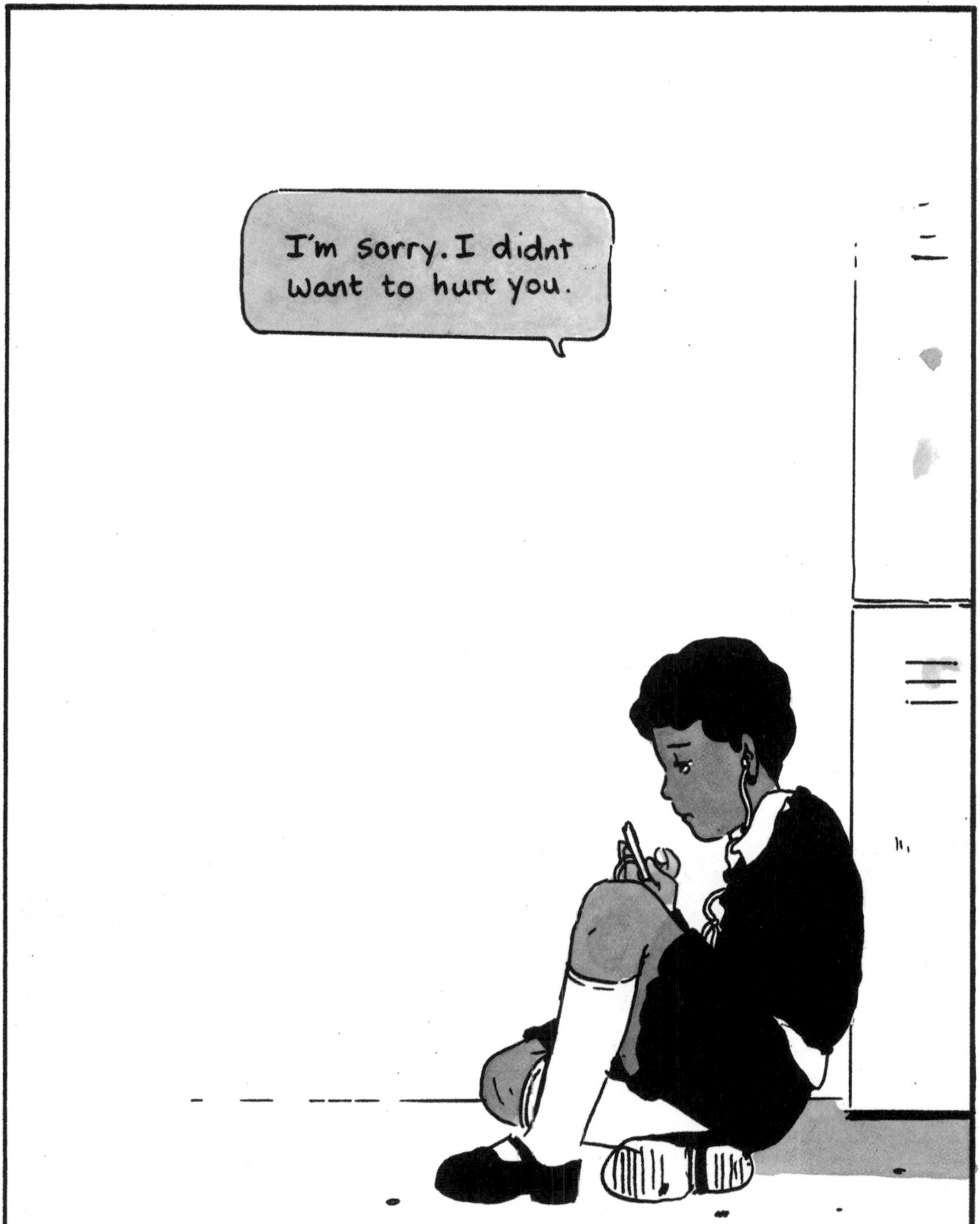
I'm sorry. I didnt want to hurt you.

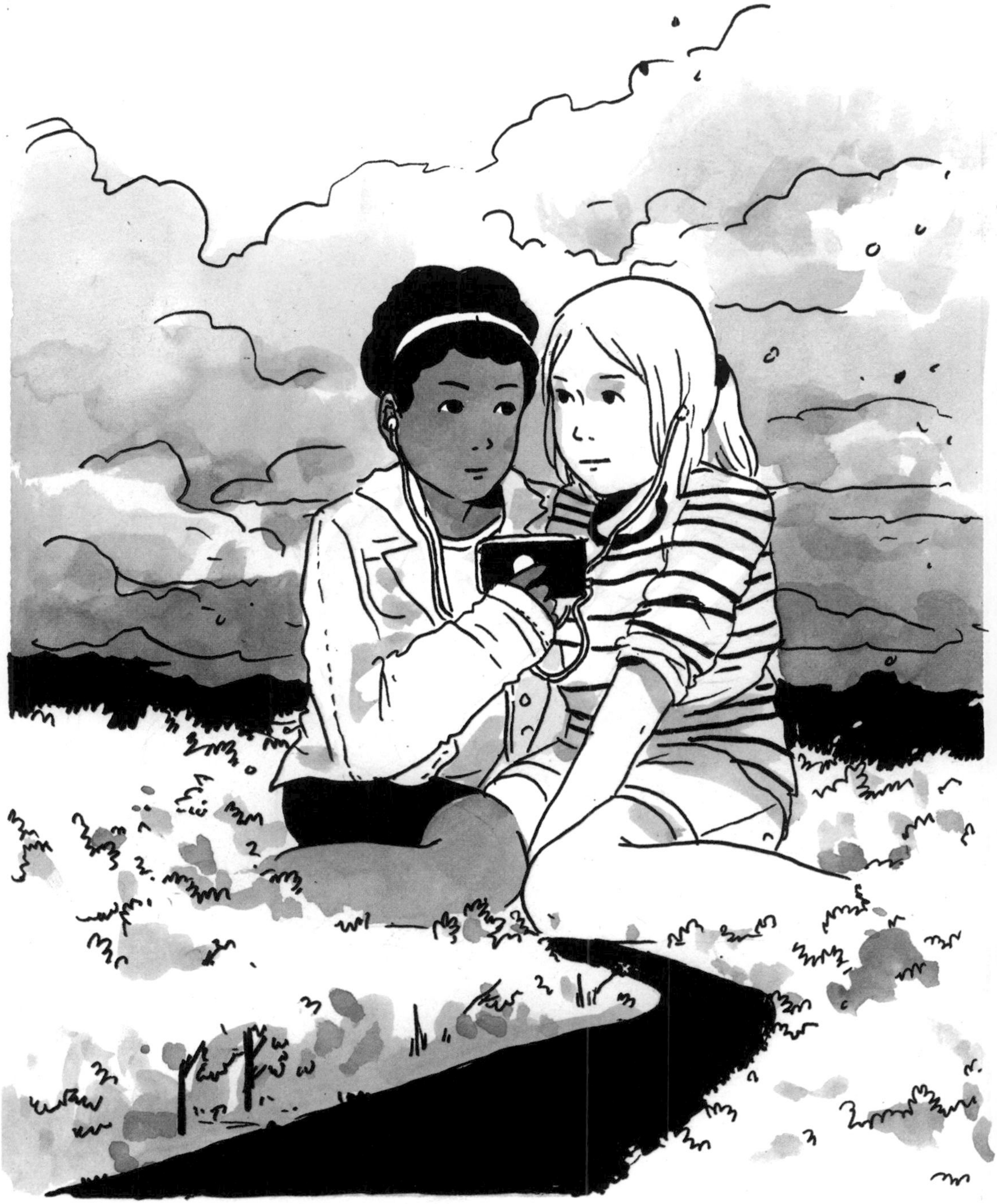

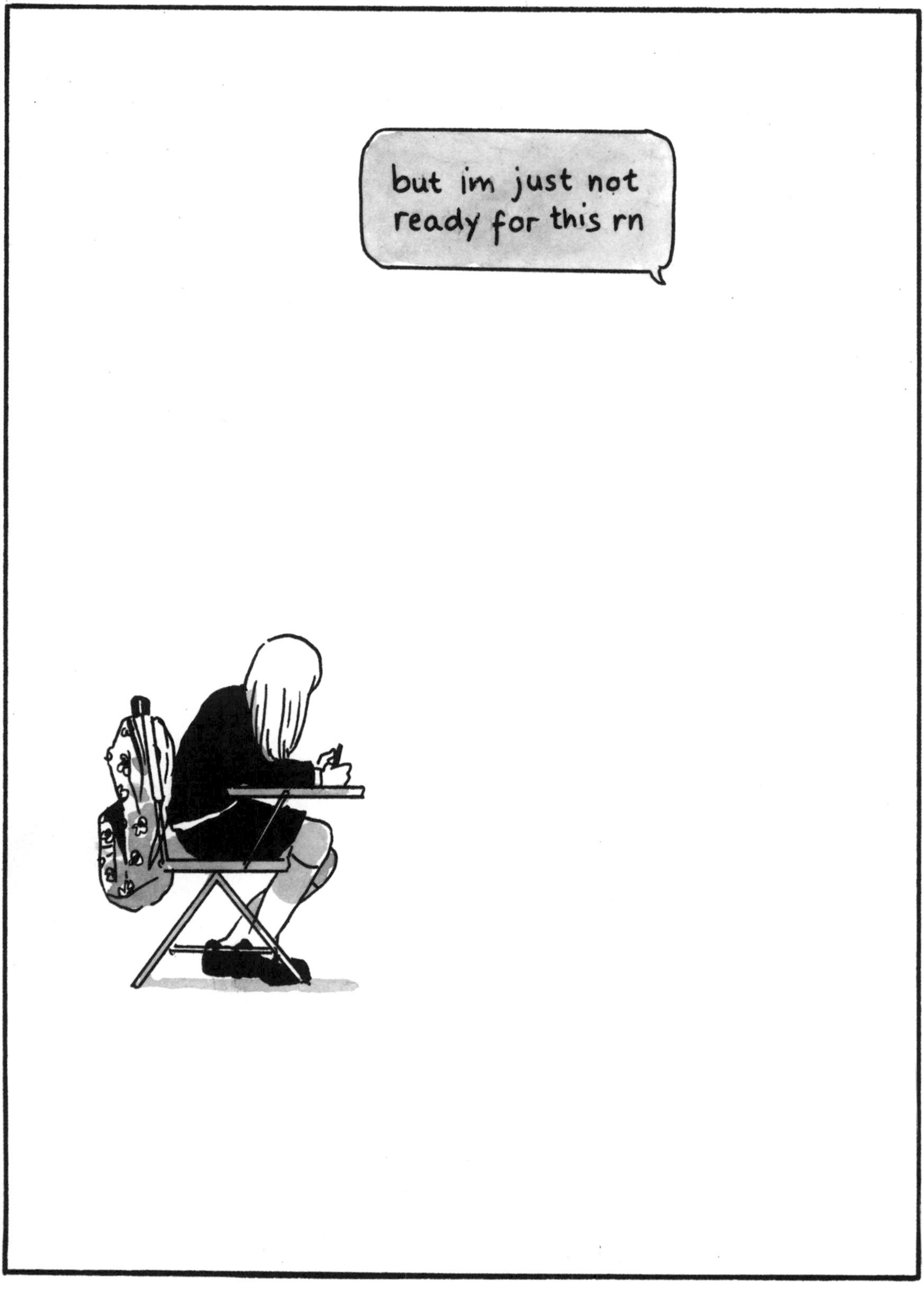
but im just not ready for this rn

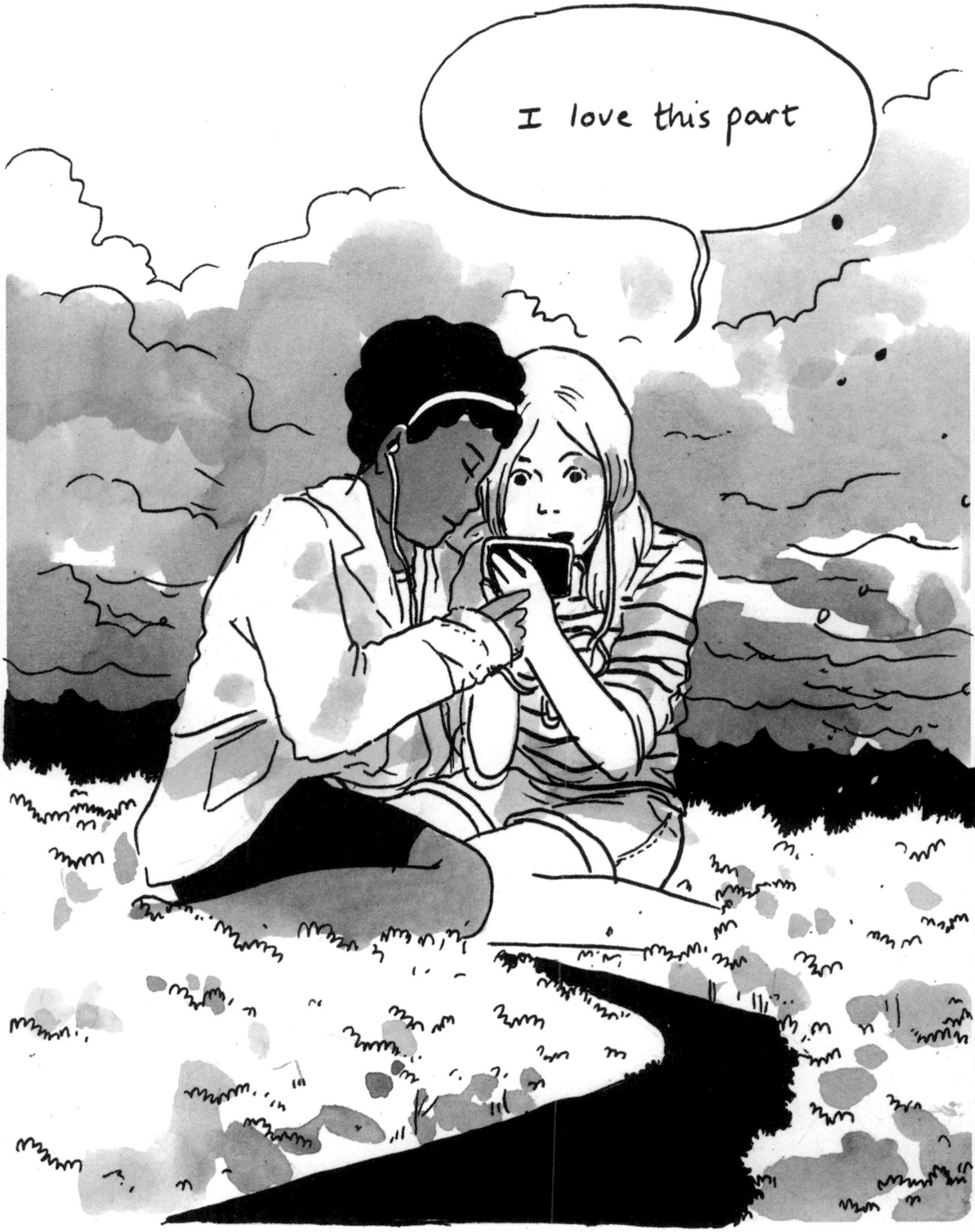
I love this part

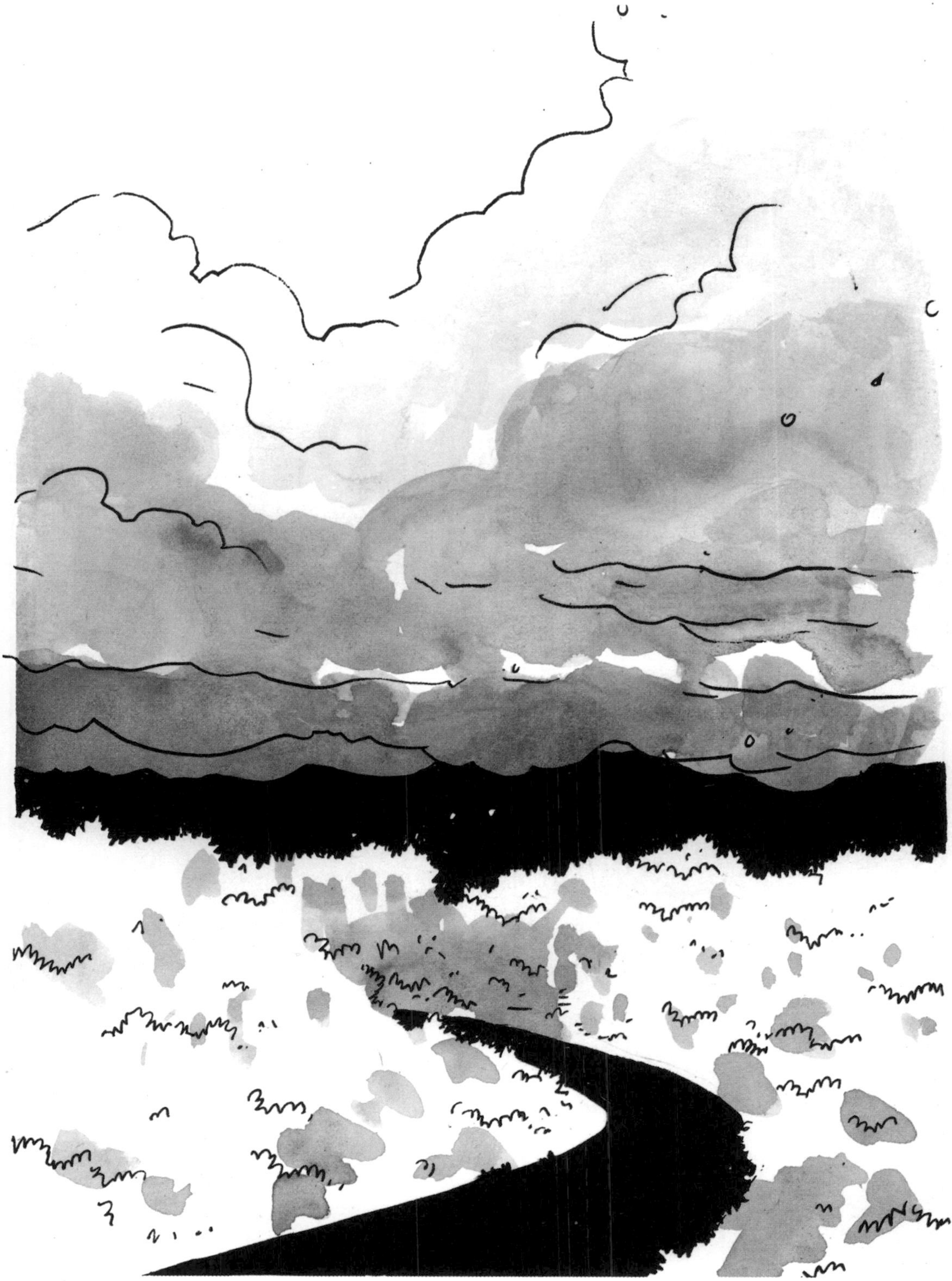

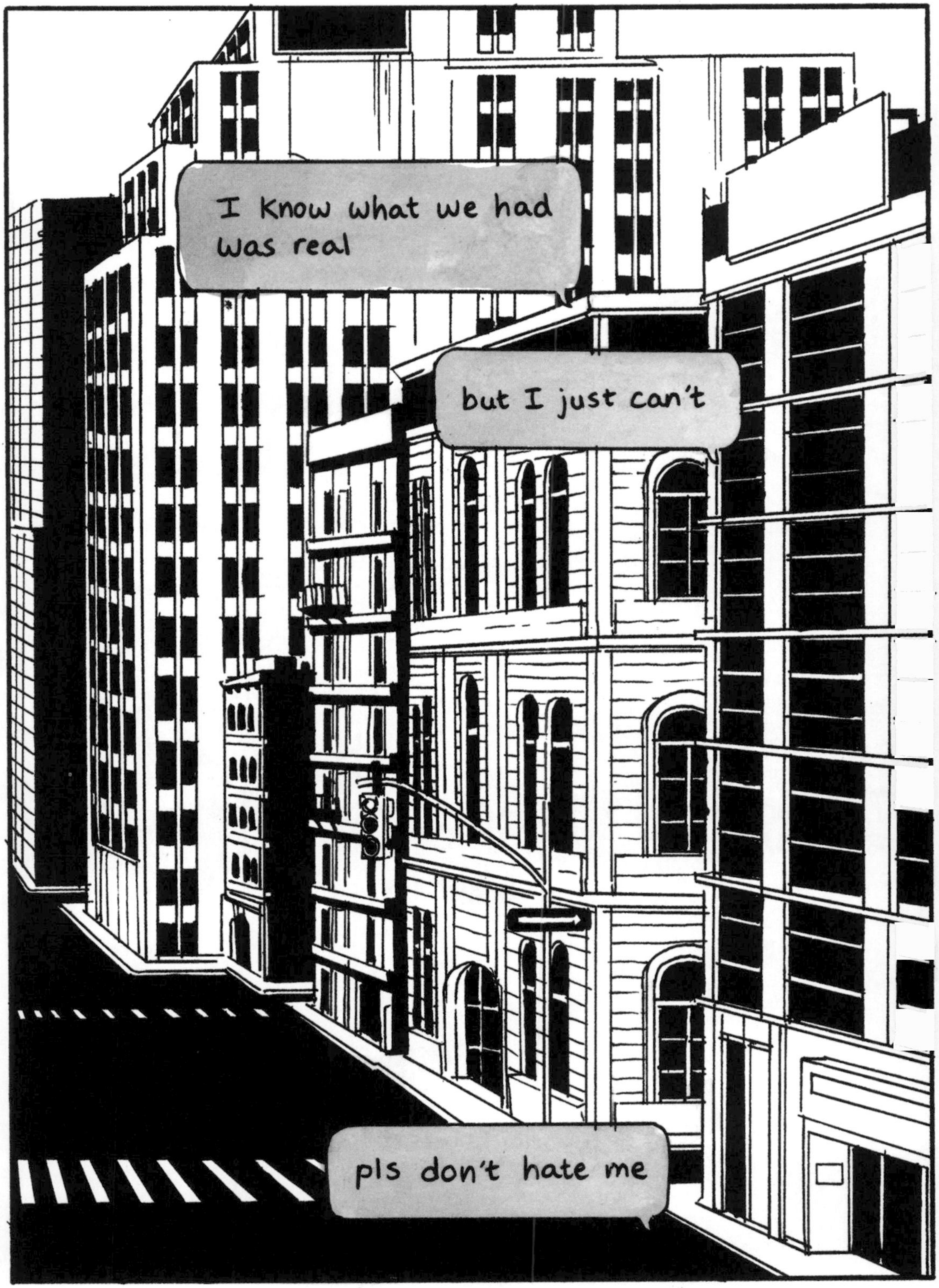
I know what we had was real
but I just can't
pls don't hate me

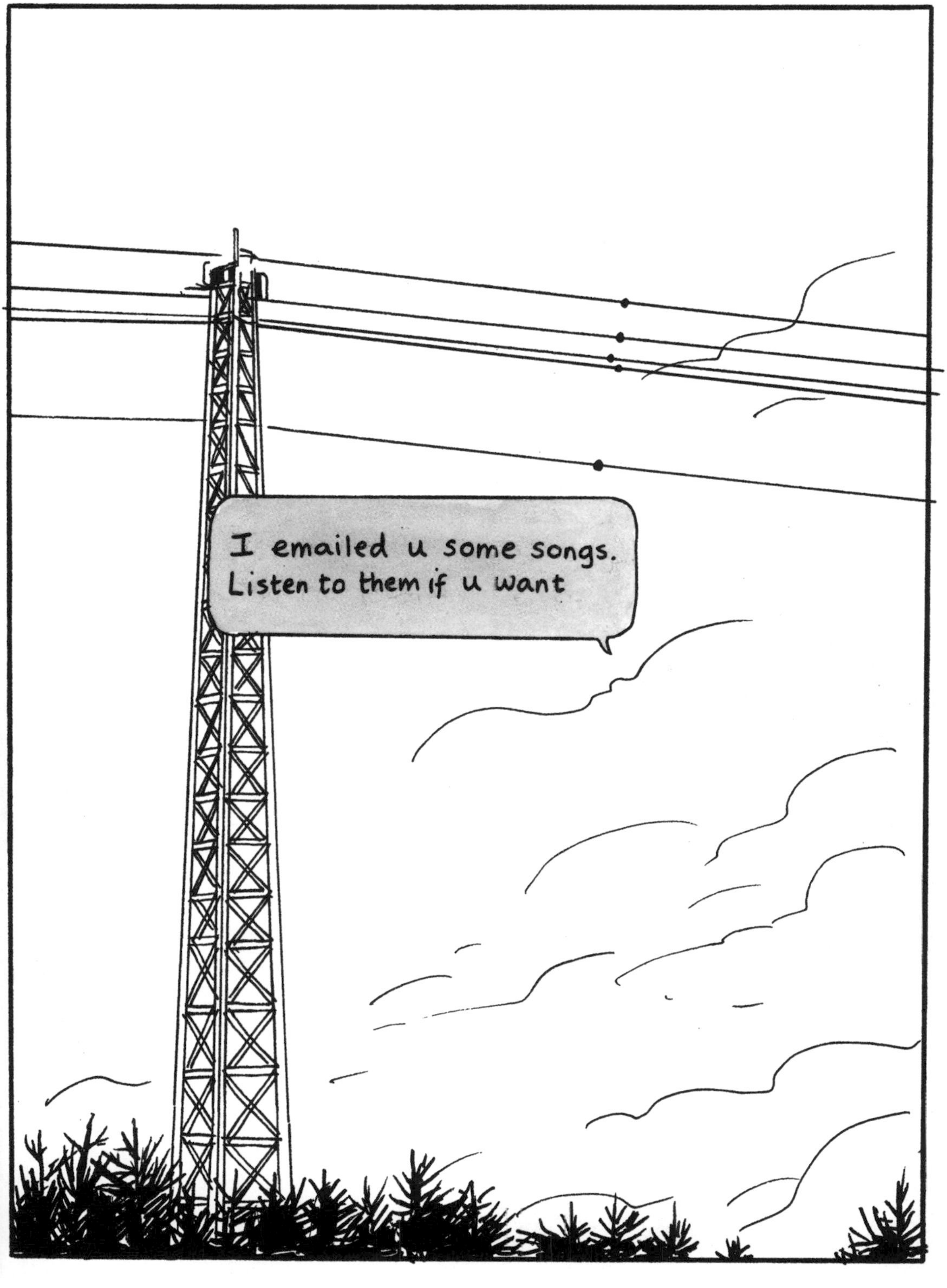
I emailed u some songs. Listen to them if u want

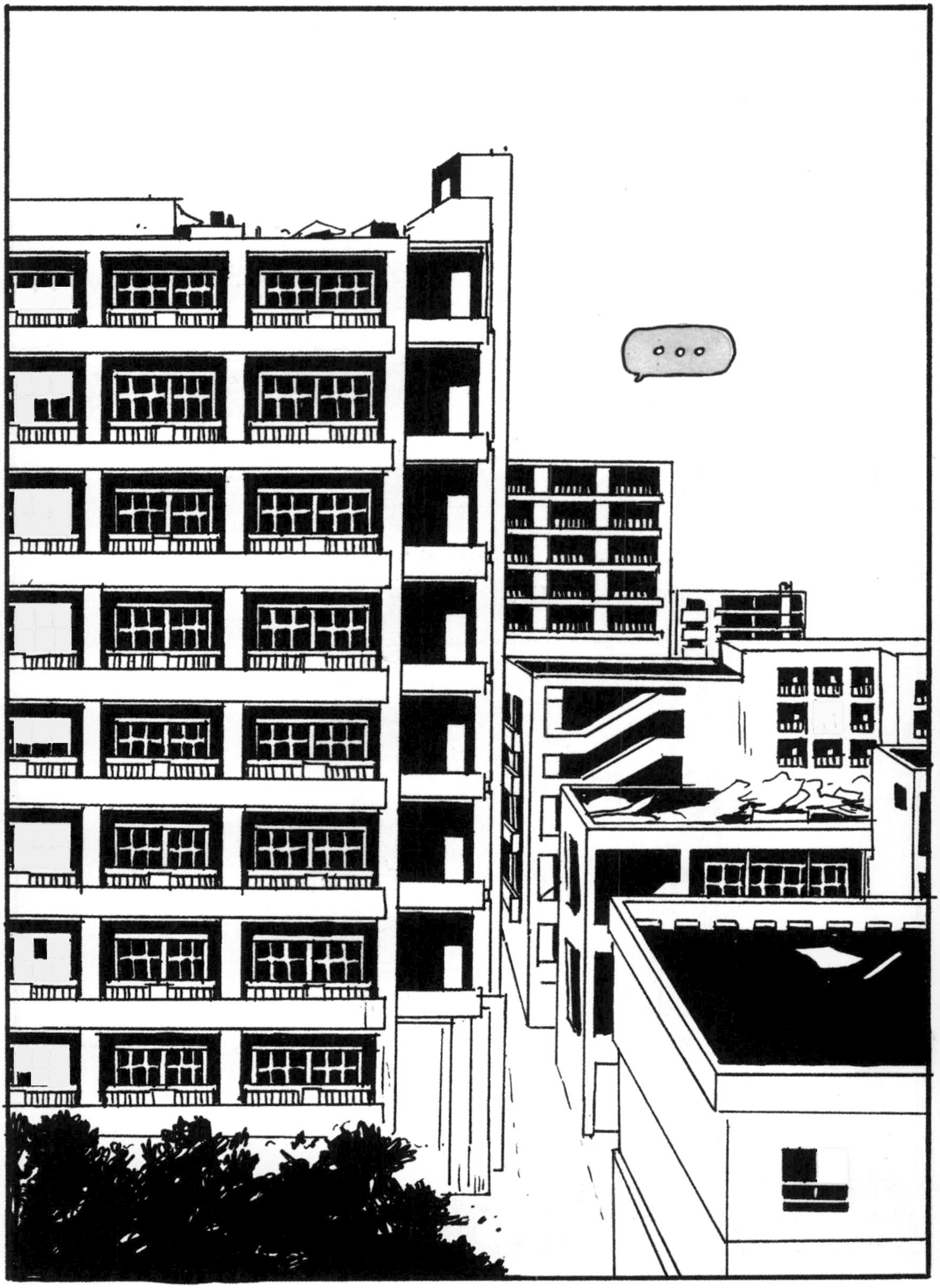
...

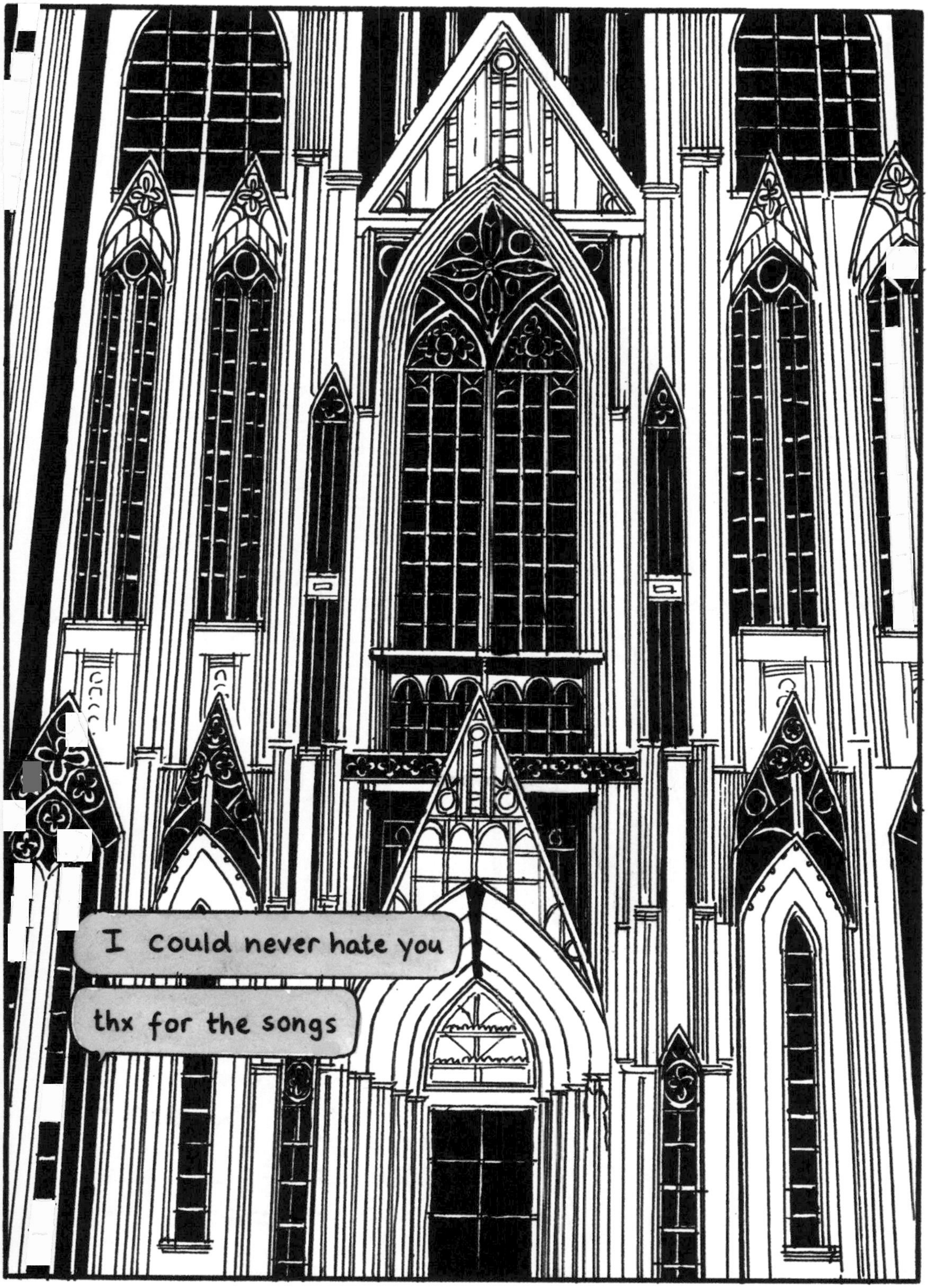
I could never hate you
thx for the songs

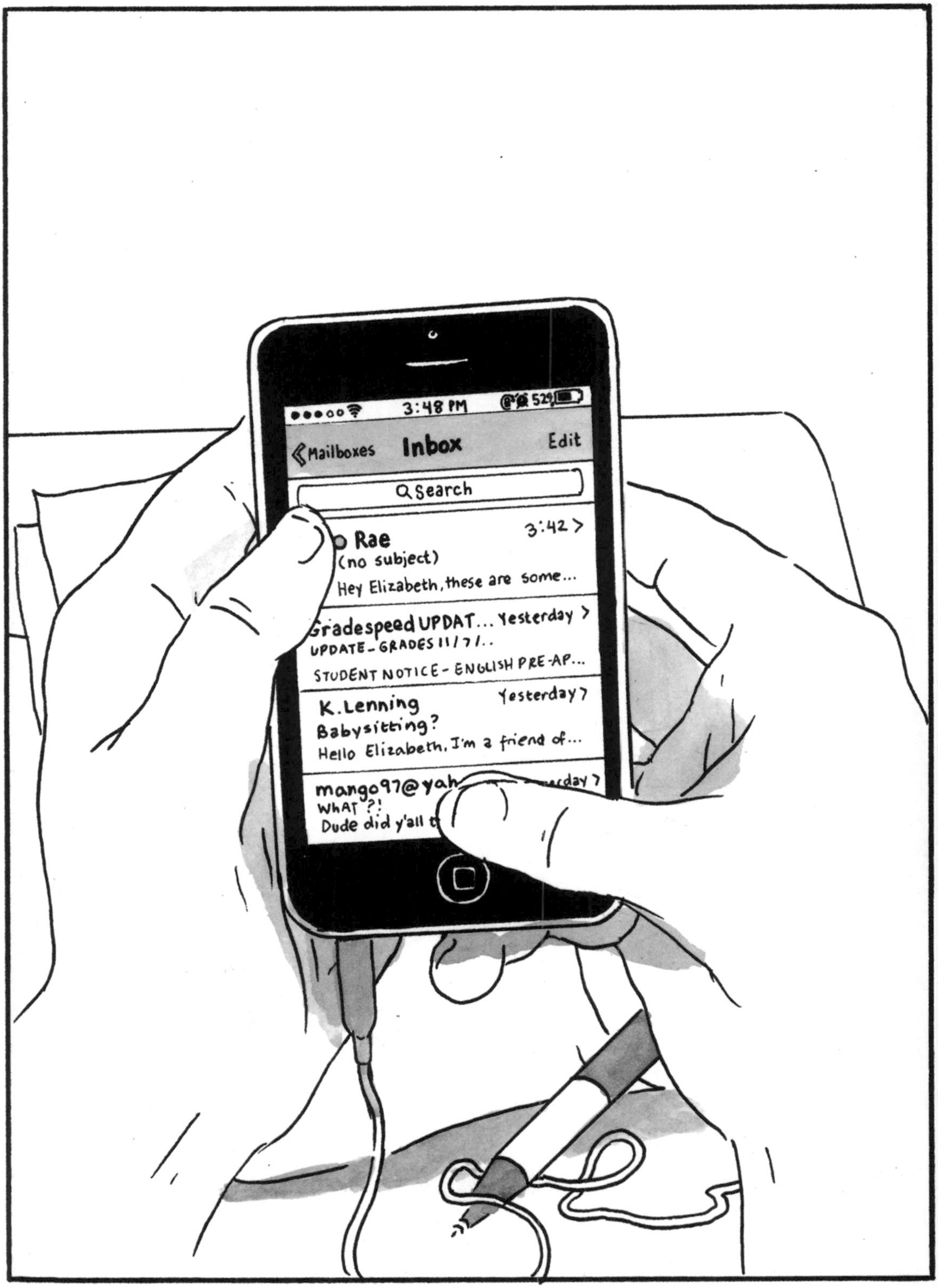
3:48 PM
Mailboxes
Inbox
Edit
Search
Rae
3:42
(no subject)
Hey Elizabeth, these are some...
Gradespeed UPDAT... Yesterday
UPDATE-GRADES 11/7/..
STUDENT NOTICE - ENGLISH PRE-AP...
K.Lenning
Yesterday
Babysitting?
Hello Elizabeth, I'm a friend of...
mango97@yah
WHAT ?!
Dude did y'all t

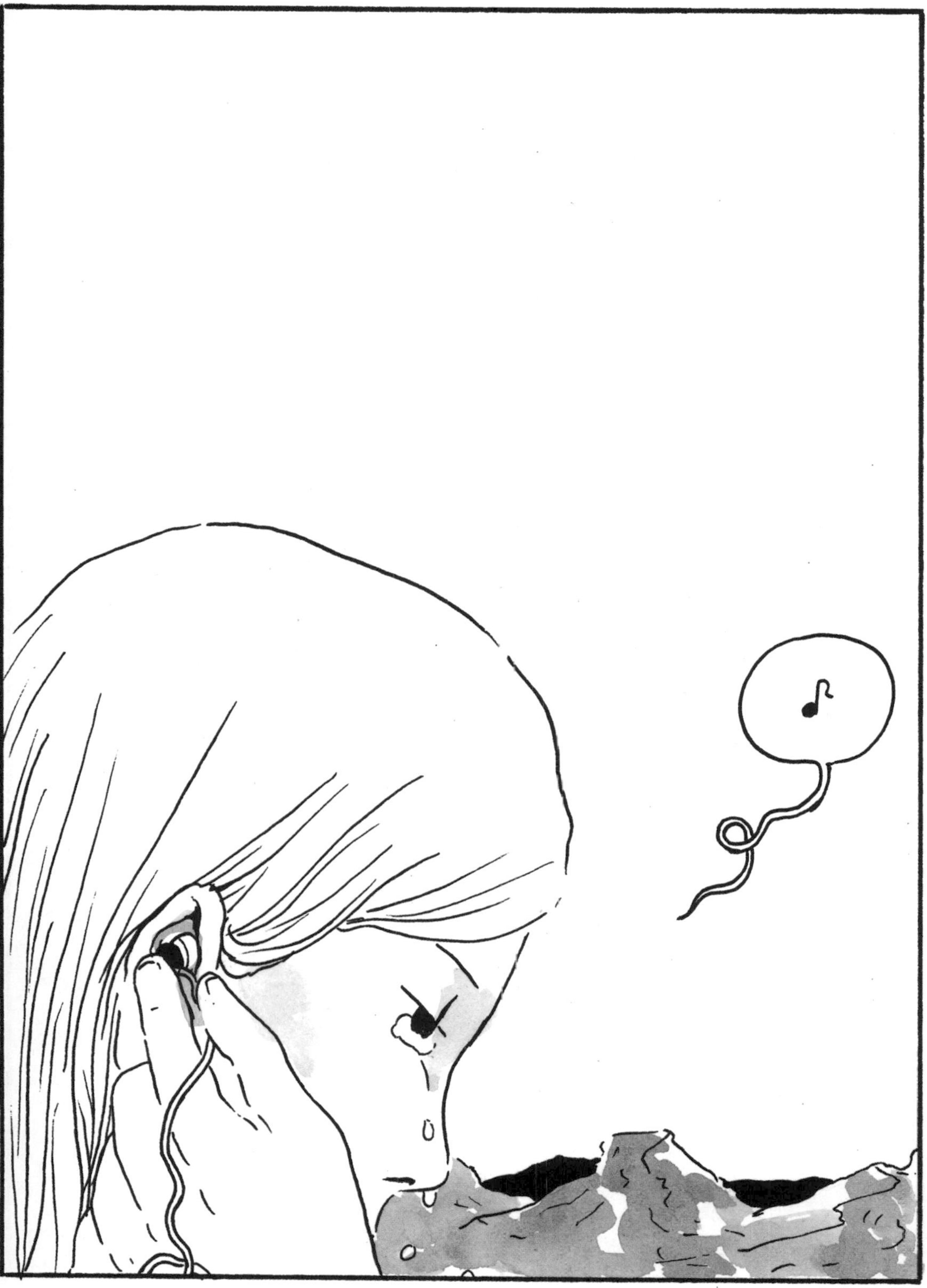

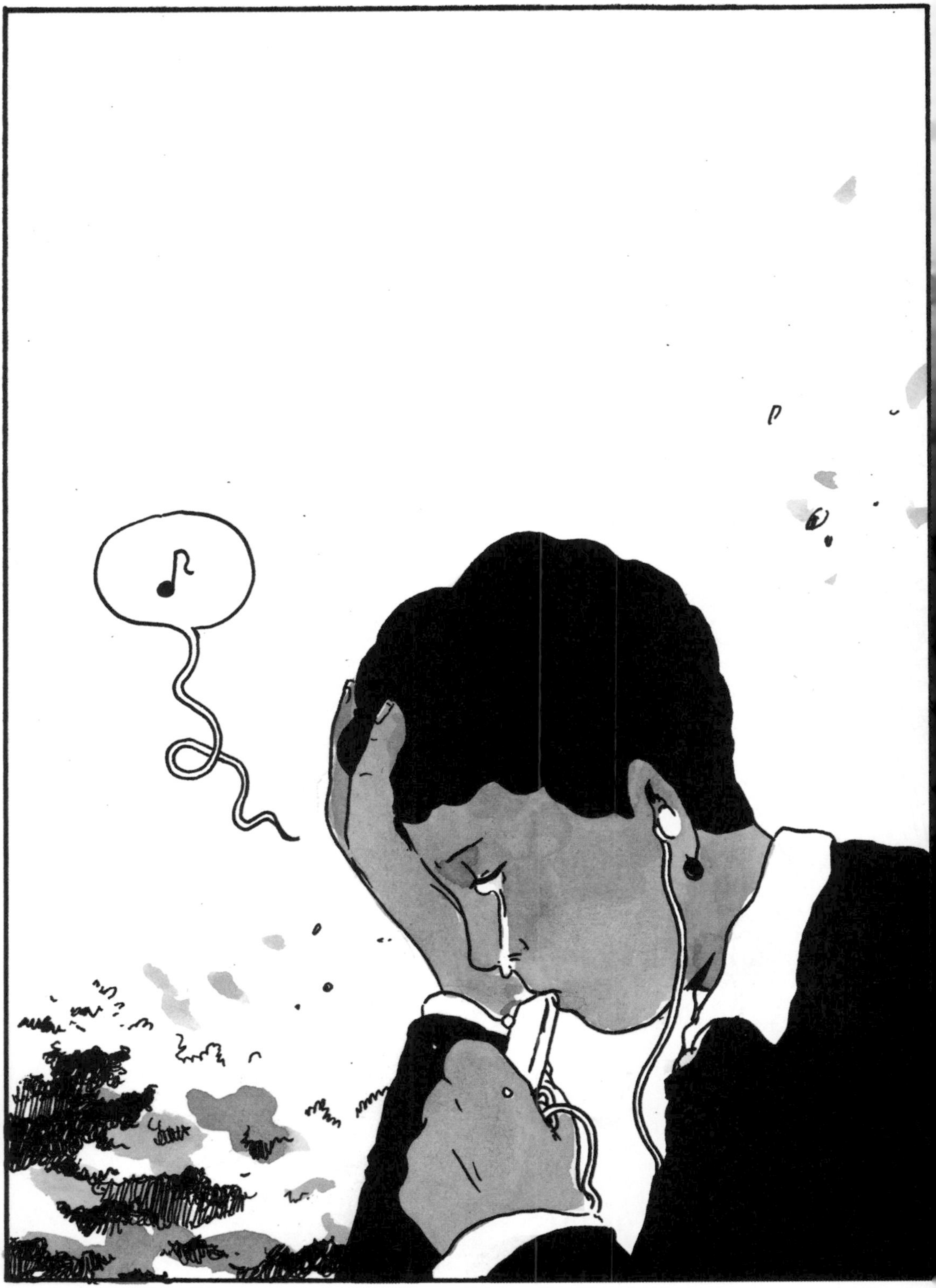

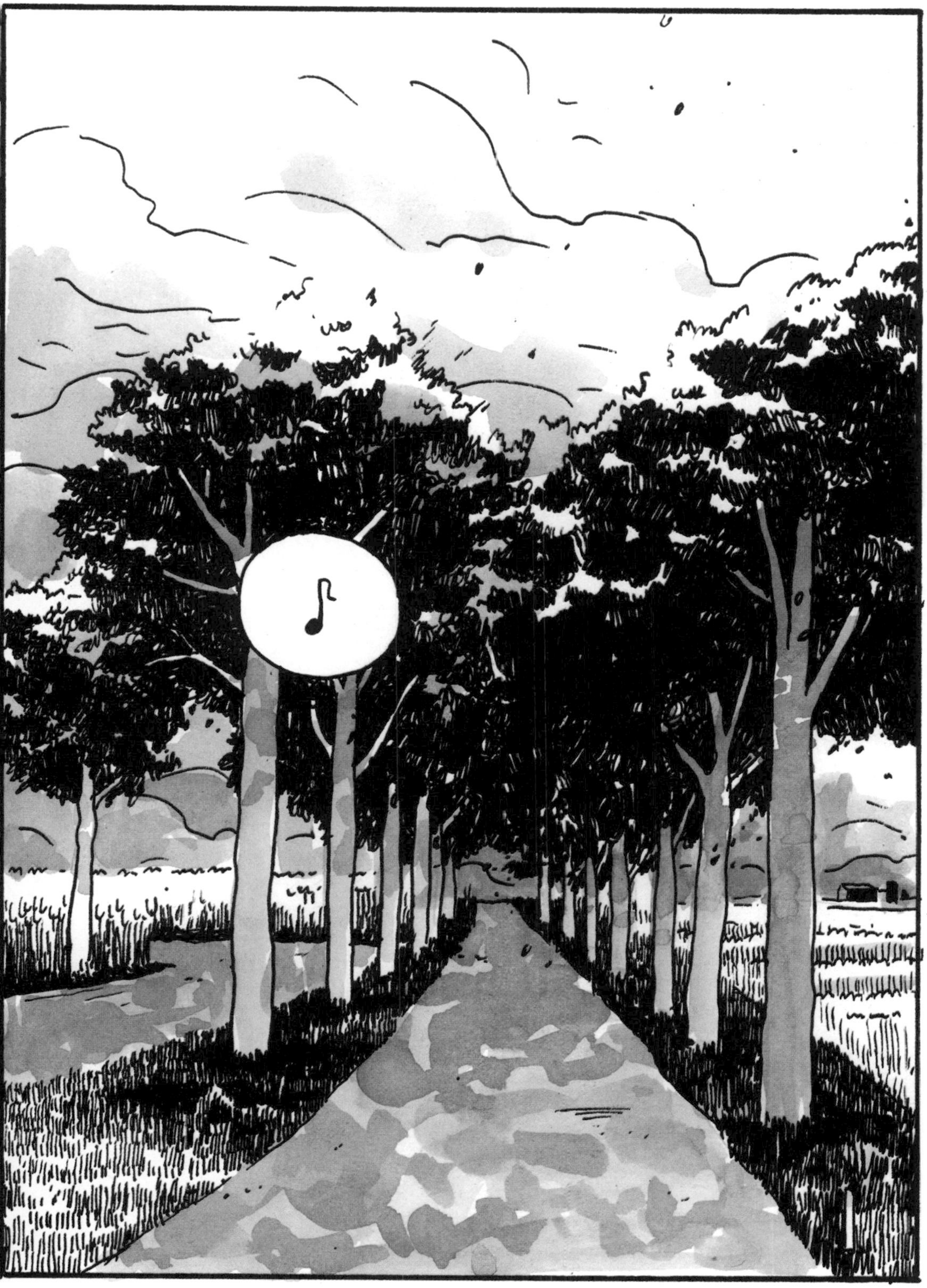

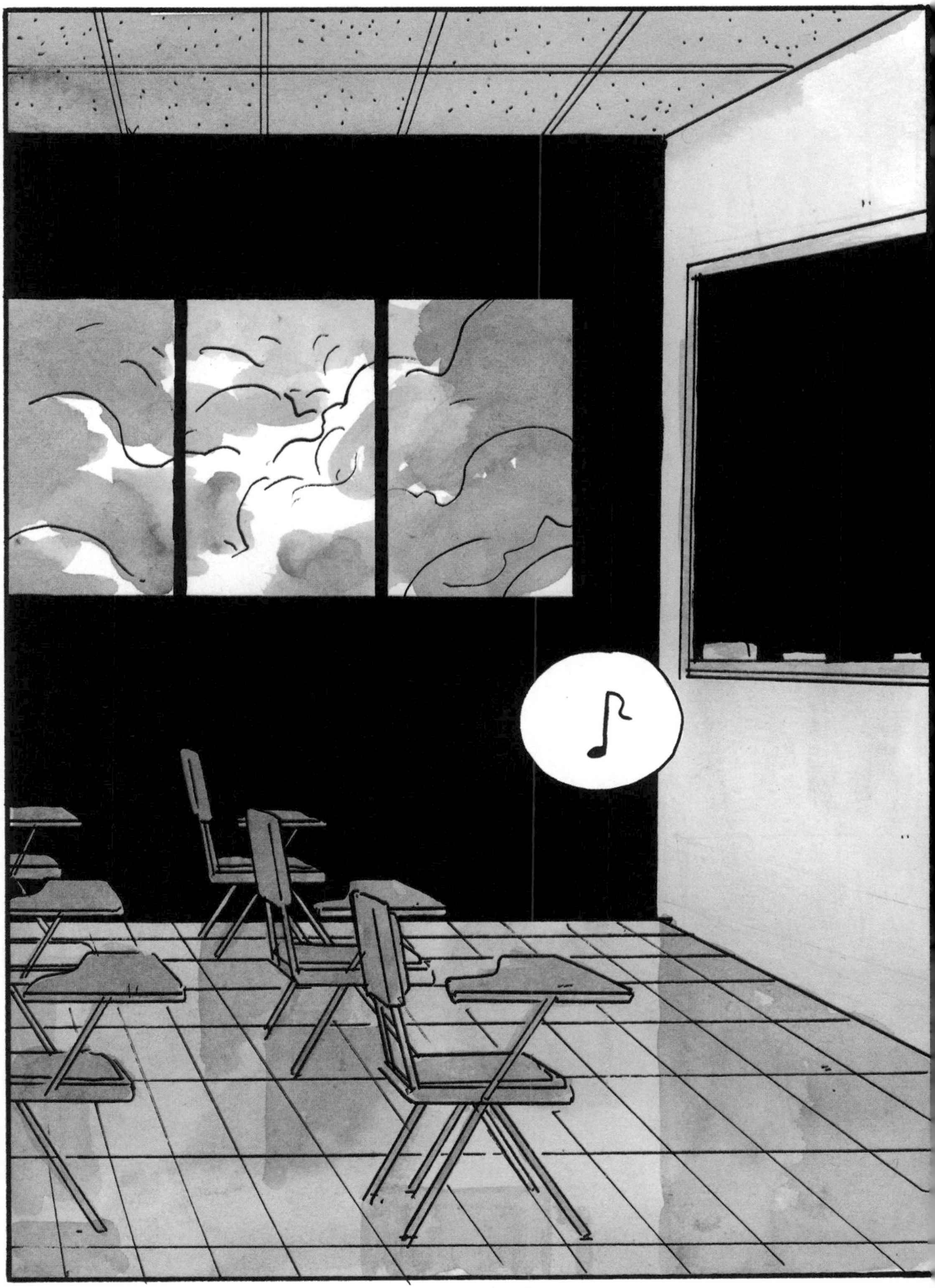

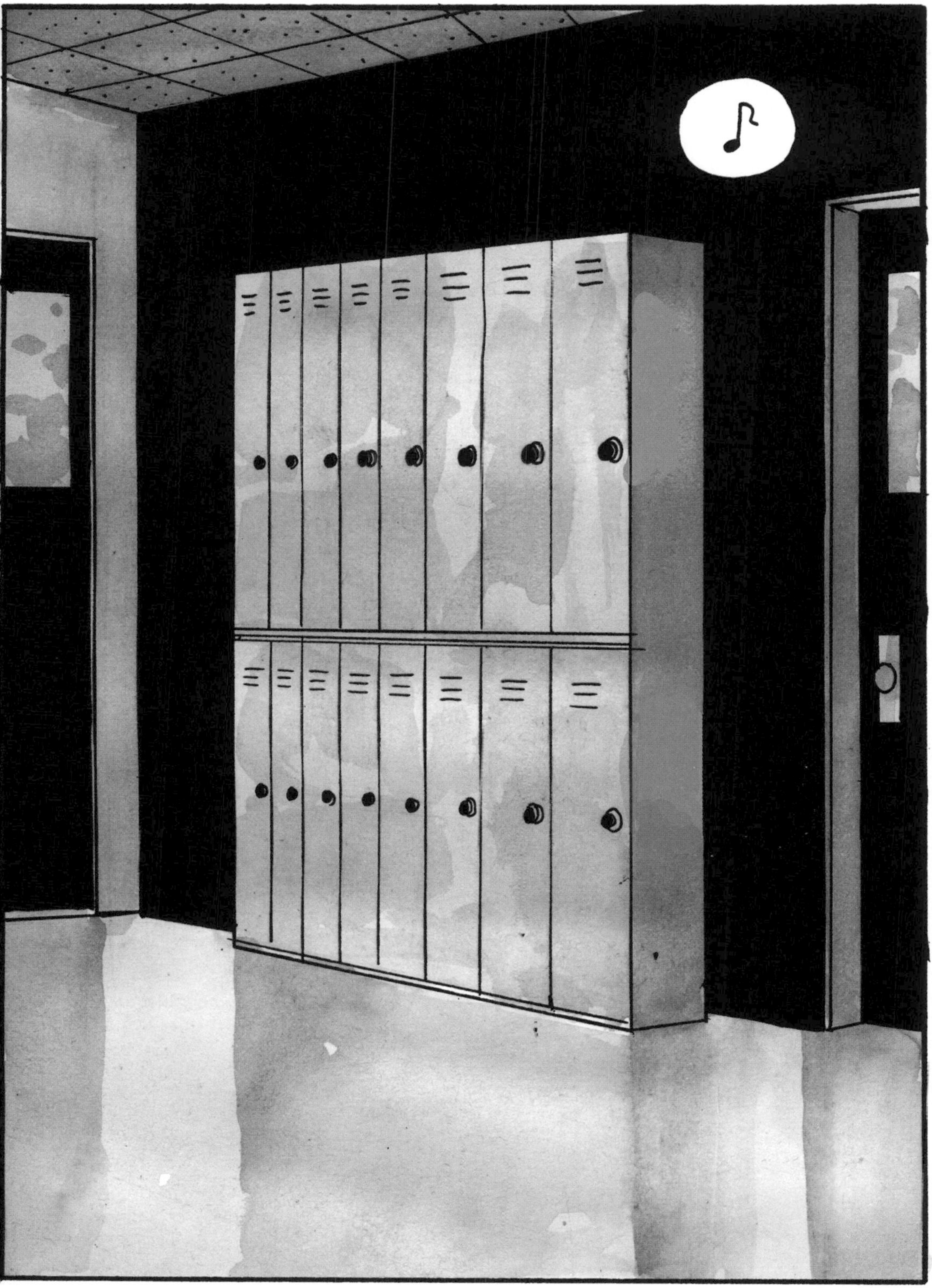

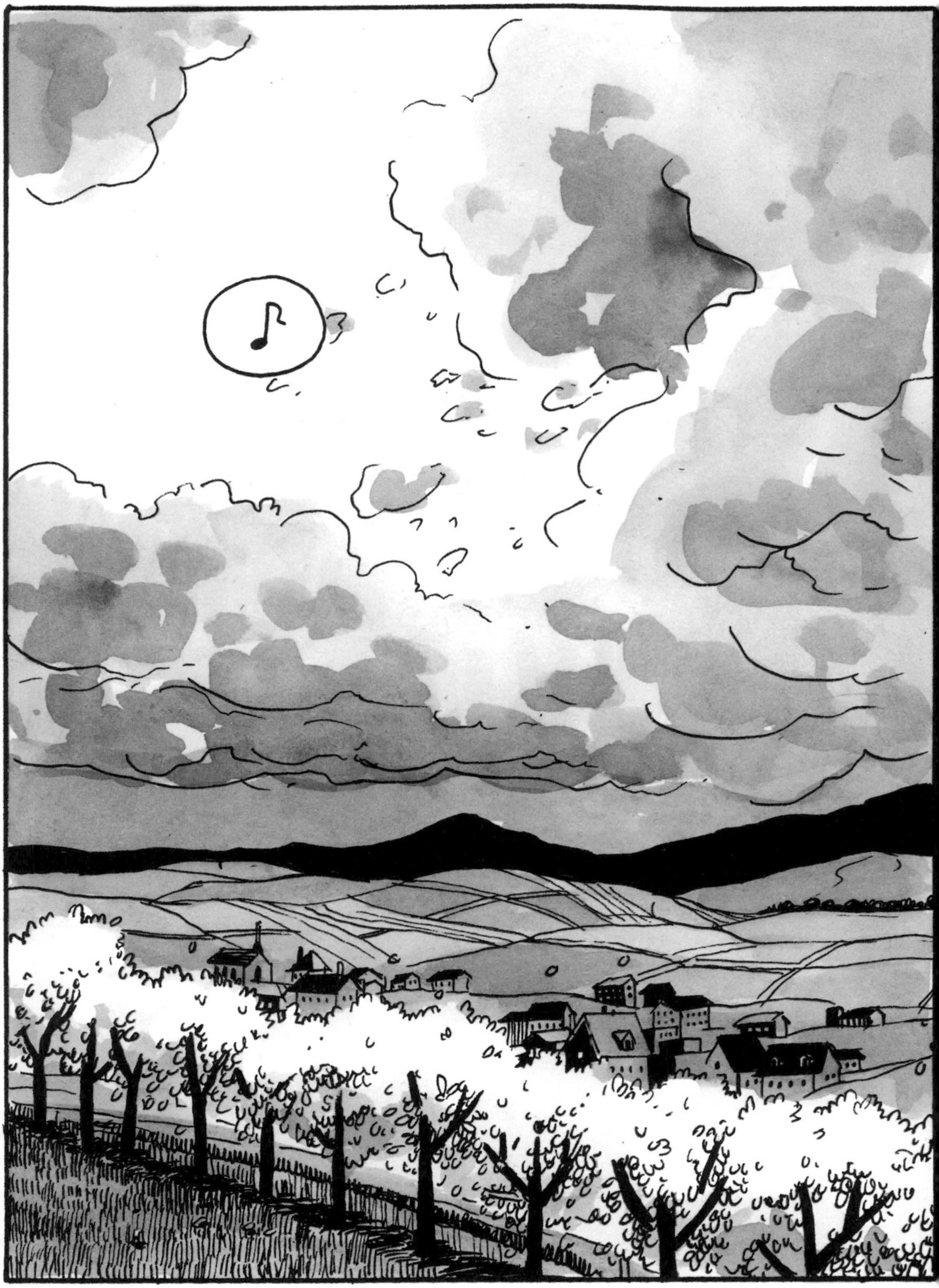

end

Published by Avery Hill Publishing 2017

10 9 8 7 6 5 4 3 2 1

Tillie Walden has asserted her right under the Copyright, Designs and Patents Act 1988 to be identified as the author of this work

First published in the UK in 2017 by Avery Hill Publishing
Office 7, 35-37 Ludgate Hill
London, EC4M 7JN

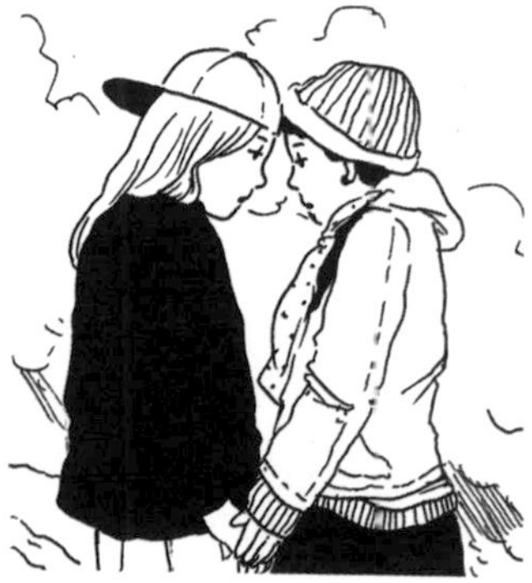

A CIP record of this book will be available from the British Library

ISBN: 978-1-910395-32-5

Tillie Walden is a cartoonist from Austin, TX. She is the creator of the Eisner nominated webcomic ON A SUNBEAM and the upcoming graphic memoir SPINNING.

Tillie Walden
www.tilliewalden.com

Avery Hill Publishing
www.averyhillpublishing.com

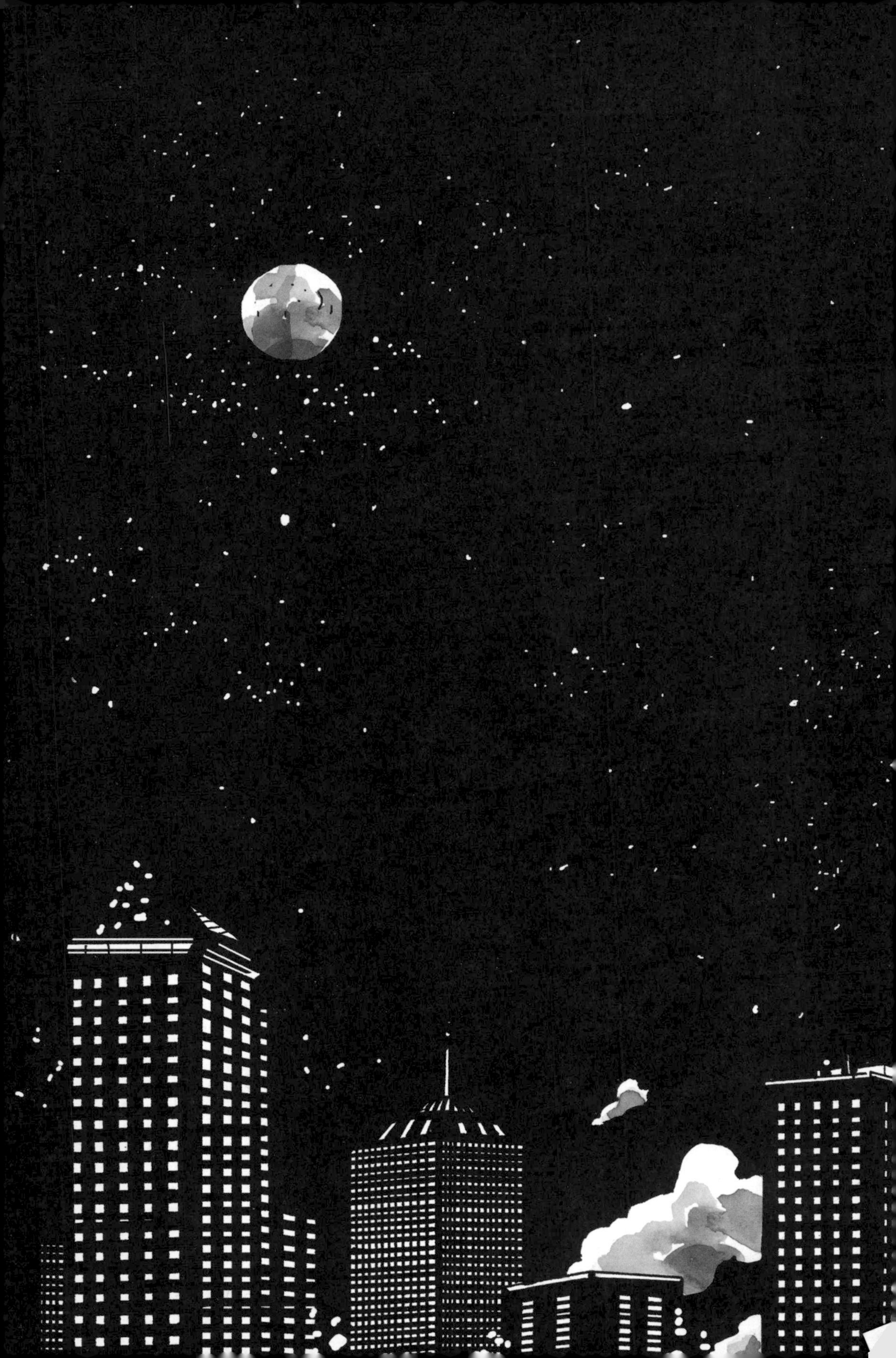